# Cathy & Jim's Land's End Walk

## March 19th to June 7th 2011

## The Diary

Dedicated to the wonderful staff of
Colchester General Hospital Breast Cancer Unit

# Cathy & Jim's Land's End to John O'Groats Walk

## We did it our way (From The Bottom To The Top)

### The Route
The place-names indicate where we ended each day's walk with a mention of just a few of the National Trails we joined

### John O'Groats
- A croft near Standtill
- Lybster
- Helmsdale
- Dalchaim
- Loch Fleet (on a reed bed)
- Tain
- Alness
- Muir of Ord
- Milton

### The Great Glen Way
- Alltsigh on Loch Ness
- Fort Augustus, Loch Ness
- Laggan, Loch Oich
- Gairlochy, Loch Lochy
- Fort William

### The West Highland Way
- Kinlochleven
- King's House, Near Glen Coe
- Inveroran (Maurice the Angler's)
- Tyndrum
- Inveranan
- Rowardennan
- Drymen

- Strathblane
- Kirkintilloch
- Kilsyth
- Falkirk Wheel, Clyde & Forth Canal
- Philpstoun, Union Canal
- Currie, Edinburgh
- North Middleton
- Stow
- Eldon Hills, Melrose
- Hawick south and within
- Newcastleton, **Scotland**
- Shankhill, **England**

### The Eden Valley Way
- Wethral
- Langwathby
- Orton

### The Dales Way
- Howgill, Sedburgh
- Cowdub, Dentdale
- Horton-in-Ribblesdale

### The Pennine Ways
- Airton
- Earby
- Widdop Arms, nr Ribblesdale
- Walsden, W. Yorks
- Diggle
- Charlesworth, Glossop
- Peak Forest, Derbyshire
- Biggin
- Osmaston (Shoulder of Mutton PH)
- Hopwas

### Heart Of England Way
- Tatenhill (Horseshoe PH)
- Whiteacre
- Knowle, Nr Solihull
- Aston Cantlow

### The Cotswold Way
- Broadway
- Winchombe
- Seven Springs
- Stroud
- Wotton Under Edge
- Horton, Chipping Sodbury
- Bitton, River Avon
- Midsomer Norton
- Walton, nr Street
- Charlton's Canal footpath
- Rockley Green, Wellington
- Tiverton
- Crediton

- St Neot
- Nancegollan
- Stoke Climsland
- Rescorla
- Blissoe
- Lydford
- Sticklepath

### Land's End
- Penzance

# Cathy & Jim's Land's End to John O'Groats Walk

## March 19th to June 7th 2011

This was and will always be our greatest adventure. I guess that is due to the 81 days it took to walk 1,008 miles while we abided by the Country Code through 458 gates and climbed 123 stiles. Oh! You thought writing a diary was banal, eh? Yes, I even counted the wooden bits on the way. You can take the old sod out of accountancy but you cannot..... account for an old sod?? Even worse is that you will discover this was not to be the saddest thing I did, I am sure, but please read on. There must be a good bit or two.

There was no set path to follow. There were some good books that gave their preferred way with suggested alternatives, but there was never going to be a defined way for us. Even the way we went sometimes changed hourly. Our general concept was a route that would incorporate the major footpaths of our land, i.e. The Cotswold Way, The Pennine Way, The West Highland Way and The Great Glen Way. Then there were the footpaths we never knew existed: The Heart of England Way, for example. So, as part of our planning process there was a big element of "What is it? Where does it go? Is it flat? Any signs of pubs?" and so on.

We decided to travel as light as possible, only taking one change of clothes and opted to patronise local eateries on the hoof to avoid carrying the extra weight of cooking gear. True anoraks can get an equipment list (if not a life).

## How could I possibly contemplate this walk: I'm blind as a bat?

My darling wife, Cathy is the reason I could attempt this adventure. Quite apart from her ability to see an Ordnance Survey map in 3D, plan, walk for ever, carry half the gear and prepare food, she can also see. Many people who have seen my Oops moments down kerbs, into glass doors, the surprise lamppost and anywhere around a dinner table involving wine glasses will stand testimony to my poor vision. *Retinitis pigmentosa* is my family ailment and a constant source of merriment that keeps glassmakers in business, so I see it (when in view) as a happy thing. Therefore, without Cathy's regular calls on the walk of, "Rock!", "Hole!", "Tree!" and many more, my ankles would have been more acquainted with plaster of Paris. Thus, the first item to be packed for the walk was my wife. The second was my diary with the ubiquitous fountain pen.

## And so I wrote on the way...

It is normally pen to parchment for me, rather than paw to plastic so I will keep this brief. I kept an A5 diary of our walk. The page size, as well as a need for sleep, restricted my daily diatribe. So be thankful. I would have liked you to see how I struggled to maintain a level of handwriting whilst flat on my thermarest bed-mat, attempting to keep the flow through an almost-upright fountain pen despite straining my already-poor eyes in the light of a headtorch. That created the further distraction of attracting flying insects to the outer canvas of our tiny tent. It was hell back there.

The page size severely restricted the use of paragraphs. Or maybe I was too tired to create them. You can invent your own whenever you wish.

I suggested scanning the diary, but my wife knew best. So, the whole thing has been typed out by Cathy in the font my PC allows and the words have been faithfully unchanged as it reflects my feelings at the time as we drifted through our evermore greener and pleasant land as the Spring of 2011 progressed. I seemed to have focused on nature's progression an awful lot, so that is what must have preoccupied my overactive brain cells at the time, although there are several interludes of adulation and insult towards my fellow man.

I have refrained from reproducing our photo album here. I hope my words are the pictures. To inflict both would contravene the Human Rights Act. The odd token gesture has found its way in, though.
Fellow walkers will know the beauty of our land. To witness it as we did was a marvel that words would always fail to fully illustrate. This did not stop me eulogising on occasions. Cathy said she can read the levels of inspiration, perspiration and desperation in my writing, so watch out.
I have generally written in the first person so far, but the whole walk was the most glorious partnership (I was even the lightweight partner, especially on the job front). While Cathy did all the work, I wrote for the two of us. The world should know that Cathy did the lioness's share of the map planning, packing and food preparation. As a man, I would want to take any credit going and will never deflect glory but, as every woman will know, the truth lies elsewhere.

## How did we ever get to agree to do this?

On The Isles of Scilly is a dastardly yummy restaurant called The Boatshed, run by Pete and his wife, Charlie Carrs. We developed all our fanciful ideas in there. Blame the rioja. From 2007 we had spent our Summers on the islands helping, often hindering, the owners of the campsite on St. Mary's. It was 2009 and we knew 2010 was already laced with plans that would not end until March 2011. But then what? We had walked Wainwright's Coast to Coast, taking 17 days over 200 miles and felt it was the St Bee's knees, so how could we follow that? Well, we could not. It stood on its own as the best varied-walk in the world. We heard that it was 'officially' number 2 to the coastal route on Stewart Island, off the southern tip of New Zealand. We went there in December 2010 to check it out: Wainwright's wins on variety. I digress. You will get used to it.
The big walk from Land's End to John O'Groats was suggested over chilli calamari. Why do they tentacle it Calamari? I am not sure

whose idea The Walk was, but I do know who must have decided we should do it. You see, when we got together all those years ago we made a pact that I would make all the big decisions and Cathy would make all the small ones. To date, there have been no big decisions.

## Did we train?

Possibly. We had always been good for a stroll and we had just over-wintered in New Zealand where we took on a four day walk or two with all the camping gear. We did come upon one problem: me. Well, my left ankle to be precise. It had been broken when I was playing footie in my late teens. They said it would cause me problems late in life. By "late", I had hoped to have been closer to the daisies than this. I also need to thank my Mum for some genetic assistance on the arthritis front. I had been getting some physio from Neil Foster, the ex-England test bowler, who said it would hurt if I did nothing and it would hurt if I walked on it, the choice was mine. Cathy saw it that she now had a complete liability to walk with. Duff at the top: in the eyes and crock at the other end: the ankles. "Why can't the middle bit fade a tad?" she pleaded. She has been looking to buy me some erectile dysfunction symptoms for Christmas.

## A happy ending?

I trust I do not spoil the read by reiterating the diary is faithful to the walk, so the celebrations, thank-you tour and contemplative thoughts do not appear at the end. The last day is the last page. So, for the curious, I will give you the end bits at the start: John O'Groats is not the true north-east corner of our land. A far more majestic place, Duncansby Head, holds that distinction with mighty rock stacks rising two hundred feet above the raging sea near the riptides of Pentland Firth where seas negotiate terms in constant disagreement. We walked there on the next morning before we took a bus to the nearest car hire company, 125 miles away. The thought of anyone in London going beyond Birmingham for a hire car puts northern Scotland's remoteness into perspective. Our 3½ hour ride revisited much of the coastal countryside we had already walked.

Rain meant there was no point taking a tour of The Grampian Mountains so, after revisiting our favourite Loch Ness B&B, we headed for a few days on The Outer Hebrides. We had heard The Vatersay Boys, a Scottish folk-rocky band we adore, were playing at The Castlebay Hotel on Bara on Friday and Saturday night so we parked up the hire car and hopped on the first available ferry. This got us in at 11 o'clock at night but it was still daylight as we pitched our tent just below the hotel. We lazed away a couple of days and jigged away a couple of nights until 2am. This was our celebration and there was no finer way.

It was a somewhat different celebration than we could have imagined. We had certainly not planned anything. Indeed, on the way, someone had asked us "When you make it to John O'Groats, what will you do to get home?"
I replied, "Backstroke."

I hope you feel with us as you read this. Please enjoy the journey. Here we go......

# Day 1 Sat 19-Mar From Land's End to Penzance   11 miles

Land's End: No sign of directions, no sign of anybody: no sign!

It was 10 o'clock and the sun shone brightly onto a calm sea. We felt the brilliant sunshine could be seen as a portent for our endeavour after the dank, cold, wet days of the worst winter for a century. Here's hoping!! Recent events were forgotten. The discovery of another arthritic joint (my ankle), Cathy's awful headache on the train down, and, just a few minutes ago we missed the bus. The taxi cost £20 but allowed us to meet Ashley, the first Robin Reliant driver to make it from here to John O' Groat's . Moidie had been the model dog and we restrained her exuberance for the first two miles by keeping her on a lead over the high cliffs towards and beyond Sennan Cove. We knew we were going to see plenty of horses, but this was our first bay. A gig trained and winter wet-suited surfers braved the bracing briny. Dog violets and celandine whispered 'spring' while their big brother, Daffodil yelled it with startling colour on almost every bank. As we left the coast a passing car stopped behind us. Simon of Cornwall kayaking ran to greet us. As our chat went on Cathy clearly thought he was Dicken Rogers (brother of our friend, Ned, on Scilly) and paid her condolences. "We are sorry about your granddad" she said. "What?" he cringed seeming to disbelieve that Cathy knew how embarrassing his Grandpa could be. I explained. Good humour broke out and we headed to Carn Brae Moor with his finest wishes. The moor, the last granite mass in our westward land, was boggy and a mite steeper than our untrained legs were prepared to smile at. A fine place for bones, though, according to the mutt. The odd horse rider, dog walker and buzzard added charm during the trek with special appearances coming from a mine shaft, a magical ancient stair-cased spring well and the 5000 year old settlement of Carn Euny, a contemporary of our B&B. Not really. Aches began after 8 miles so we discovered sitting down. We also discovered a local who could not give directions to her home town which we could all but see. Moidie only snapped at one dog and snarled at another. She is too knackered now, even to whisper 'spring' as loud as a celandine.

## Day 2 Sun 20-Mar from Penzance to Nancegollan   12 miles

Last night's monster moon '30,000 miles closer to humans than normal' provided a spring tide that transformed Mount's Bay and Penzance harbour from high-and-dry to brim full over the six hour course of our walk. How did we know? We walked away from the coast, didn't we? Well, we returned in Graham's car to pick up Scott's car at the end of the day.

Scott and Di may be 14 years our junior but are kindred spirits in their sense of the alternative. They have no house but own a boat often seen in St Helen's Pool at the Isles Of Scilly in recent years, hence our friendship through the Hash House Harrowing experiences. Graham is Scott's Dad: a sprightly 74 year old. They arrived at 9-30 outside Con Amore B&B under grey tranquil skies that barely changed all day. Smartly into both walk and cordial conversation, we rattled along the two halves of Mount's Bay: either side of Penzance's Docks. The tide was dropping fast on the shallow slopes of the beach and we breached the sea defences at the first opportunity to stride out on sodden sand with the castle on St Michael's Mount just out to sea ahead of us. Yes, we could see ahead of us. Coffee and photo shoot at Marazion gave a breather before we took to the lanes. We had apologised for today's terrain, the route was so bereft of grassy tracks, but over lunch in a field of daffodils, Scott enlightened us as to geocaches. We were soon ripping Di's legs to bleeding shreds on Godolphin Hill to the point where she would have gladly remained on roads all day. At the apex was a big boulder: surely the place for buried treasure! The ladies pulled away loose stones beneath it to reveal a chamber just the size for a Tupperware container full of trinkets. We wrote our hello, dropped in our secret gift and refused to take anything on the grounds of travelling light. Our descent found the grassy track our tootsies had been missing then rejoined the lanes aligned with yellow bulb fields. Graham's car at Nancegollan heralded the journey to Newquay ( St. Mawgan) via Penzance (told you). Moidie's adulation was followed by dinner with Joan (Graham's wife with her electric cigarette) and Eve (S and D's 11 year old twitterer). What was the secret gift? The geocache book on Godolphin Hill reveals all.

Accommodating Folk: The Tallins: Graham, Scott & Di (Joan was busy not smoking)

## Day 3 Mon 21-Mar From Nancegollan to Bissoe 13.5 miles

The Tallins continued to excel after a fine night. Scott pointed our creaky joints east out of Nancegollan near the 'Porkellis 4 miles' sign, having driven in mist for us to resume under a lightened sky. Our resumption also included a rucksack, just one, whilst Scot's home retained half our load for our eventual return on Tuesday night. The rucksack was my new one. A Berghaus C7, I'll have you know. It squeaked. Each pace generated a high pitched "eek". So much so, Great Tits competed. Why were the birds calling? Because it was spring? No, to out-sing Beardy's bag. Once again the traffic free lanes provided direct routes for us through the Cornish scenery. The changed industrial scene now had bulb fields surrounding tin mine wheelhouses; the grass carpeted Cornish banks (not one ATM in them) and the proud Kernow flag for Cornwall's independent claim. We crossed several hills and vales through classic landscapes with a couple of chaps pulling over their vans to chat once they had seen the Land's End- John O Groat's sign on our ruckies. Cheesy chips proved too much of a temptation at the Golden Lion around the top of Stithian Water. Or was it the Tribute Ale? The sun had poked through by the restart, enough to get me down to just a T-shirt. Of course, it had been shorts all the way for me. We had come north of the reservoir as the only footpath cum bridleway we took had been deviously redirected onto another route preferred by a farmer. The disguised detour turned out to be marching orders to the north. We were not to see the wonderfully imaginative name of Perrarnaworthal on a village sign, so Frogpool became its substitute. We checked here for buses to Constantine to save Zanna Jeffries the longer fetch, but no go. When I rang there were two screaming kids in earshot ( screaming in excitement, not thumb screw screaming ), so it was a more placid Zanna who toured Bissoe and Wheel Jane to finally find us once we had emerged from the welcomed cuppa at the Bike Park Cafe. Just by the arsenic works, a dying industry. Tales of her husband Dougall's last working month filled the granite house in homely Constantine. The quirky house is so much 'them 'and very much us. Hake and ginger joined wine and olives as conversations flowed particularly of New Zealand's shared memories and Dougall's dodgy knees.

**Day 4 Tue 22-Mar From Bissoe to Ladock   12 miles**
Cathy's lost lens added a spectacle to the departure from Zanna's, who kindly dropped us off at Bissoe Bike Centre. We had lured the lovely Zanna (pictured showing all the directional sense of Mark Thatcher) to Cornwall's interior where randomly sporadic lanes must, from the air, resemble a bag of Bombay mix. Convincing each other that our legs 'were getting into it', we climbed steeply past the Wheal Jane reservoir to turn north easterly on a rural byway. Three

buzzards wheeled effortlessly upwards on a morning-sun generated thermal spiral. It was 6 miles to Truro along peaceful lanes with deciduous trees that hid the conurbation until the final moment. Sainsbury's provided new glasses for Cathy and a phone call regarding our home-mail from Royal Mail Redirection Services who said that the Shaw's house (circa 1750) does not exist. Further confusion from traffic enticed us to miss a turning, the first of three errors of the day. Pasties while sitting on the Jehova's Witness Church wall fuelled the climb out of Truro and its grand sandstone cathedral. The Kenwyn area of the city was leafy with period houses. Its church had an extensive cemetery with mature trees leading down to country fields via "The 40 steps" said our engaging local, "there's 129 of them". Errors 2 and 3 occurred either side of idyllic Idless. Nothing extensive but the effect was cumulative to a hilly day's walk. Idless wood was our first woodland walk thus far. With much of the forest without leaves, it was light and airy, but its serenity was interrupted by Paul Cull's phone call, often fragmented by weak signalling; about his legal battle for the odd million or two quid from McAlpines that goes back to 2002. The rise in blood pressure pushed me to the rise in contours. There were a lot of these. Primroses helped. Their pretty faces and gentle colour were a psychological massage of our calf muscles that were beginning to tighten. Zanna's fruit allowed me to have a date with Cathy in the church lobby in St. Erne where lactic acid set my calves to stone. A rusty waddle out of the village found us with a Mancunian of Indian descent walking 2 miles home from the bus after a day's training to be a nurse at the age of 36. This age, accent, colour and activity in this area were charmingly engaging and we never stopped chatting. We could not accept his offer of hospitality as Scott was on his way for our Laddock rendezvous, so we pressed on over the final 2 hills. The Tallings hospitality continued to be as boundless as my appetite for pizza.

Oh, today also contained the first chiff chaff as well as the lady who stopped to wish us well happened to be the neighbour of dear friends Andrew and Hilary Julian in Perranarworthal.

## Day 5 Wed 23-Mar from Ladock to Rescorla 13 miles

We continued to receive carer-therapy from the happy Tallings on a soft, sunny morn, and then Scott drove us back to Ladock for the uphill start. Once, or finally, on top of the highest point we were head on to an easterly wind that hung around all day. Trees and vales defended us for the most part while still veiled in sunshine. Moidie had begun the day as stiff as a drystone wall. This generated the possibility of us getting a hire car from St. Austell and transferring her to Katie's at Bristol. By lunchtime it was _our_ groaning bodies that looked for a retirement home. Moidie would press on alone. High white stone viaducts converged from the countryside into the suburbs of St. Austell while we endured the gauntlet of the pathless

A road into town for half a mile. China clay mountains of spoil towered above the area but so did our next hill, which made the descent into the town centre a tad disappointing. Recompense came from Walkers Take-away and Restaurant. Pies and chips were comfort food to supplement our healthy fruit bars noshed earlier (thanks to Di). Steepness followed. The church spire was soon below us, then much below us. We aspired to even greater height but so did the noise of the traffic. This added to growing fatigue which was partly helped by a lady who fetched water for us without us even asking. How lovely. So was the lane away from the broad rat runs. The tiny hamlet of Roscorla rested on the eastern edge of a high hill with monster china-clay mounds just over the valley. Just before we got there we realised we had forgotten the dog food at the Londi's shop half a mile back. God bless Cathy for doing the extra mile. Our hosts at Yazuma's were a sensitive happy couple who loved Moidie. This couple were in their 50's, just and both male, just.

### Day 6 Thur 24-Mar from Rescorla   to St Neot   16 miles

Fruit and the full English enabled this army of two to walk on our stomachs all day. Almost marching at some stages. Two separate stops around Bowling Green allowed well wishers to fill us in with local history and gossip, despite our attempts to engender brevity. The sun was bright in the sky and cheery primroses were stretched open to bursting point. We were walking well. Maybe we had cracked it. I was experimenting with two poles. My left ankle was still weak on rough ground but I was free of pain for most of the time. Cathy had devised a way around most of the hills which hit the succession of Celtic crosses on the Saint's Way that acts as the oldest route through Cornwall, the Coach Road. It is now a peaceful lane. Cathy only needed a tub of ice cream for lunch at Landhydrock Estate where the National Trust maintained the grounds in impeccable style. Through its northern woodland for a mile we went before confronting the inevitable contours nature had developed leading up to the Bodmin Moor massif. At the base of the steepest valley was a notice that at first, sank us. "This bridleway is closed after damage by flooding....... there is no alternative route......" The orange mesh fence blocked the way. I don't think we ever contemplated turning back to engineer the extra miles around this hill. We pushed round the fence and crashed through the landslip, steep though it was. The hill was the hardest to date and went on for 2 miles. We emerged to a verge and phoned the Sturmers with a rendezvous 4 ½ miles further on that we doubted we could reach. Yet we did, even though two of these dastardly miles were over the moor proper. 16 miles and only one minute early. Colin arrived on the dot and it was soon Tribute time with Janet's lasagne. We fell asleep thinking about the thin horse. Not under fed, just narrow, as if a proper horse had been split between nostrils and ears then made to look right again. A slice of horse. Most odd.


**Day 7 Fri 25-Mar From St Neot to Stoke Climsland    13.5 miles**
Too full from last night's feast for too much breekie, I finally completed the digestion process by lunchtime. My eyes had been too greedy for Janet's fine fare. The steep start up and out of St. Neot got the system going. Cathy was in good form from the start to the finish while I was ready to nap at the drop of a map. Great sunshine blessed us again as disused chimneys and fauna kept us busy. A ninth century king of Cornwall, King Donliert had left two engraved stones on the edge of Bodmin Moor that would have had wooden super structures on them. Mysterious and yet the perfect place to grab a lie down. The moor proper opened in a few places to give the Big Country feel to the day. Moidie just welcomed the chance of a bit of rabbit. We stopped at Minion's tea shop for a sandwich and drink with just a swift moment or two for shut eye. The descent from Bodmin Moor meant the remaining hills were to be easier if not less prevalent. That last one into Rilla Mill was as steep as it could get. With one moor to the rear we felt we could define Dartmoor over the

next, smaller ridges. Our route through Upton Cross and Bray's Shop led us to Stoke Climsland while we discussed Colin and Janet's wonderful wedding story and got bombed by a low flying buzzard. Savoury rice dishes, raised bubbly and bon ami flowed until our eyelids dropped. Lovely Sturmer-land!
Text from Scott to Cathy: "have got a pair of your knickers, shall I post them on?" Cathy's reply: "keep them as a memento." Scott's retort to Cathy:"I am wearing them already."

## Day 8 Sat 26 March From Stoke Climsland to Lydford 14 miles

The day started with bacon sarnies, bye-bye to travelling Janet, £23 for two pairs of socks then Colin dumped us at Stoke Climsland for our 2 ½ mile descent to the River Tamar, the Cornwall /Devon border. The steep down was a prelude to a different shape on the other side of the valley. Steep at first, the more gradual slope lasted for 3 miles before flattening out. Boosted by a call from Mark Underwood and an ice cream from an out of season ice cream farm (12 minutes of rustling in a barn for stock) we strode out between the characteristically groomed Devon hedgerows. Today's roads were straight with one pointing in the right direction for three miles past Brentor's high church, stuck a couple of hundred feet up on a lump of rock. Closer to God I guess. A hamlet with air but no obvious G string sat under Dartmoor. This was Brentor whose old station showed that there is life after Beeching once enthusiasm and paintbrush are partnered. We joined the West Devon Way to enjoy the soft turf beneath our feet all the way to Lydford's boundary. Above the village, the evening sun had caught the white dead grass on Dartmoor's broad back to form a lunar landscape at full moon. The steep down and up to Lydford proper was a sting in the tail. Talking of tails, we had just seen some curly ones on some Cornish Black pigs on the outskirts. I nearly bagged a brace. After swearing every six steps out from the gorge, the square castle loomed large beside the pub carrying that name. A historian measured 12 ½ poles from footpath to footpath as I took ale. Yes, Lydford, like Wallingford, was laid down on the 12 ½ pole system. Well, I never. Back to the Tribute for a glug until Colin arrived. Back for bangers and gravy at the Whitchurch Inn.

## Day 9  Sun 27 March From Lydford to Sticklepath, Okehampton 13.5 miles

Further heroics from Colin saw us outside The Castle at 9-15 after the clocks had gone forward. The local hotel was too posh for mars bars but happy to make sarnies after breakfast. Cathy smiled but left as the Granite Way needed our footsteps quicker than that. This old railway line kept on a level bed whilst all the hills around had lost theirs. One land owner wasn't playing ball so a detour found us in the Fox and Hounds Hotel who donated crisps for our cause. Round a bend, a mad driver overtook at speed, nearly hitting us. Swear words and curses of painful death were hurled at his exhaust pipe. Rejoining cycle route27, the Granite Way hugged us to Dartmoor then enclosed us in granite cuttings and sent us over two high viaducts that straddled valleys. The largest being Morden, the longest metal viaduct in the land. There were more chiff chaffs on our way than we could shake a twitcher at. Coal tit, nuthatch and merlin were worthy of note though. As was hot chocolate and cheese scones  at Oakhampton's volunteer railway station. Cathy did lots of widdles. It was a notable Widdle Day. We had been carrying our donated crisps up our jumpers so at widdle stop 74b, Cathy's control of crisps was similar to that of her bladder and there was a meeting or sprinkling. Salt and shake or something similar. The weather was fine although the easterly was stronger. Colin reckoned it was 1,000 feet in altitude so maybe that was it. In the sun it was gorgeous. The 4 mile path from Oakhampton, through woods and fields to Sticklepath was the final delight of our best day's walk so far, in terms of ease. Are we in danger of getting fit? Just perhaps. Moidie had a day off with her Uncle Colin. In Sticklepath we saw the only water-wheeled powered foundry and a set of stocks. Lucky for me, the stocks were locked. Then Colin and his new canine companion arrived to whisk us back to watch a lawn mower assembly and eat curries at The Ganges while Colin told us of the highland ram that ran at his range rover. "Dong" and out.

Perfect hostess Janet Sturmer showing her lean side while husband Colin is looking stocky.

## Day 10 Mon 28 March From Sticklepath, Okehampton to Before Crediton 14 miles

Happy 1st Birthday' Ashley, the day we saw our first swallows of the year. Dear Colin dropped us at Sticklepath stocks on our 10th day of perfect weather. The local stores reopened that very day so we dutifully loaded up with pasties. Cathy was in fear of her sniffles developing into a Jan-like cold (? That sounds odd, but you know what I mean: a cold like Jan had). I took as much weight as she was prepared to give but I could tell the day was much harder for her. Well, until the "bastard" hills of Spreyton got my buttocks over-worked. I've never felt those muscles do that before... This was `Fly` Spreyton on account of some dead being- or `been` laying under the cricket changing rooms since stumps last September. It was also the starting point for Bill Brewer, Jan Stewer, Peter Gurney, Peter Davy,

Daniel Widden, Harry Hawke and Old Uncle Tom Cobley and all. The song was sung as badly as yesterday's hymns, culling two foxes, a warren of rabbits and forcing three squirrels to fall out of their trees. Only our hearts were harmonious. So was our annoyance, though, once we found the futile hill before Yeoford. The valley we had followed for a few miles on a carless leafy lane was left to meander alone with not even a footpath to follow it. Lots of basst'ds (my chosen term when I was annoyed with a hill). Woodpeckers (greater spotted) and buzzards attempted entertainment but hatred of hills filled our senses. Then the pointless downhill to the pub we knew was shut. Yet, nay. The lady at the Mare and Foal was stirred by Cathy and, admiring our plight, served us with orange and lemonade and all the packets of crispy things the bar had to offer. We all but fell asleep in the garden but roused ourselves against the tide of the school run to a campsite on the edge of Crediton, home of St. Boniface. Well, he wasn't anywhere we could see him. The farmer believes we are doing this for charity, so we will donate the fee to Breast Cancer Research. It was 5-30 before we had the pasties, Lovely. The dear tent welcomed us in. Moidie loved it. By 6-15 we had become cocoons entwined in our new sleeping bag inners that topped up the season rating of our duck down bags. We ducked down into them and they worked a treat. We did not emerge as butterflies, but 13 hours in bed must have generated some beauty sleep. The last train woke us at 10-30pm which meant the 8-30 and 9-30 did not. In the dead of night the resident 100 sheep flocked round us. There were baaas, maaars and the lamb's eeers very close to our ears. In tiredness we did not know what to do other than send Moidie out. A simple clap of the hands did it, although this created a stamped which the tent was lucky to survive. Only one more wake up. Some twit, the Tawny owl (I think it was the female) that gave a too-whit as it flew over us calling until her distant mate too-woo'd his guiding call. The first showers fell overnight, too.

## Day 11 Tue 29 March From Before Crediton to Before Tiverton 14 miles

1 hour walk into Crediton; 1 ½ hours breakfast. The cafe donated a cherry and walnut cake (rescued from their bin for Moidie. Sod the dog, we had that. A new 11 registered van stopped. He had cycled LEJO. He donated 2 bananas and a bar of chocolate. Outside Morrison's a 94 year old sprite of a lady tried to give cash. The barmaid at Bisley Mill printed the weather forecast and campsites in the area (including a nudist colony). Only the route was less than kind. Devon never got the hang of going round hills. Even the Exe Valley Way was over the hills and far, far away. The clue was in the name! Valley, so why put the way over hills? I renamed it the Next Valley Away Way. We were too high to see the Exe for 3 miles. Not that the low cloud permitted any view from the heights gained around Shobrooke and Thorveton. Blackcaps and green woodpeckers called, wood anemones and blackthorn emerged but, sadly, so too has the nettle. Resting has become more selective as a consequence. With no settlement for three miles into Tiverton we were short on camping ground. The sewage plant was not an option. Our only chance was a 100 roomed Georgian mansion; Collipriest House in very private grounds. An elderly lady who owned one of the apartments said *she* was trespassing, strictly speaking, by just walking on the lawn. The owner was a grumpy man, but the one to be asked. Persuasive Cathy strode on. The 60 year old had guests and two springer spaniels. Cathy played on both. She kept talking while he looked to refuse, mentioning our love for our great country until he granted us special use of the daffodil-strewn hill, as used by badgers and tawny owls nightly.

## Day 12 Wed 30 March From Before Tiverton to Rockley Green, Nr Wellington 16 miles

Our first day of walking in the rain, our first canal, flat walk and niggles. From a drizzled daffodil hill, our sodden tent was carried into Tiverton's `eat` bakery where we found two full breakfasts and two empty brains. We found our own way to the canal then realised I'd left half a tin of Chappie on the bakery shop front. Who looked dumb then? Drizzle turned to rain then back again. The south-westerly began to get onto our backs for the first time in 12 days. Swans and moorhens were new adornments, too, along the flat towpath. I pushed on at a pace Cathy mistook for fitness, I was hurting enough that I wanted to get this over with. Precipitation persisted until Sandford Peverell, some 7 miles from morning tent pegs, at around 12-15. We resumed at 1-00 and sun shone at 2. By 2-20 we were at Barlsford where a pub failed to appear. When it did it had no accommodation, then the Poacher's Pocket 1 ½ miles on had accommodation but no inclination to take dogs (or humour) or give a favour (or a smile). We were so annoyed we began bickering. Cathy's left leg had been hurting every step for 3 miles and I was just as knackered in the ankle/foot department. It was our least happy day. Yet another dog-refusal failed to help. We walked for further than we had planned with only the sight of a hunting sparrow hawk as scant consolation. Finally, 3/4 of a mile before Wellinton, our 16 mile limp ended at the Old Vicarage B&B. Tea, showers, tent on the line and ice on the legs all helped to bring us back together.

## Day 13 Thu 31 March From Rockley Green, Nr Wellington to Charlton Nr Taunton 13.5 miles

Heavy rain passed through the night. The same could be said of sleep. Fully fried up, we posted excess socks and bits back home then set off at 10.15 once we remembered the map that had been left on the B&B ledge. We soon gave Wellington the boot and headed north east via Pool and Ash, onto a byway that was the muddiest track since Tiger Feet (or was that Shawaddywaddy?). At one point I fell face-down. I was walking on a ledge of (what I thought to be) firmer mud above a monster tractor-tyre trench. The edge was undercut. I did not know that until I drove my stick into it and leant on it, mid-pace. The stick shot through the rip-curl, down into the trench, swinging me violently right and forward. The heavy rucksack gained momentum. My right foot gave way, gravity took over and my nose found mud. It did not take long for Cathy to laugh. Then me, too.

That 2km track took an hour to pick through. We took umbrage at the drizzle peeing on us after that so we popped into The White Horse at Bradford on Tone. One last drizzle fell along the Tone valley before broken sunshine proved April begins tomorrow. The river led us into Taunton and the canal led us out. The Bridgewater and Taunton Canal gave us a flat route, passing west-to-east under the M5, to our night's resting place on its bank outside Charlton where we had mainline trains in close attention while Moidie became similarly disposed with the local farmer's randy dog. Enthusiastic, too. It swam across the canal just to get a sniff as well as the classic Moidie rebuff.

## Day 14 Fri 1 April From Charlton after Taunton to Walton before Street 17 miles

Crossing the western main rail line was another big tick. This took us from The West to The East Dene Way and from the canal to a mature River Tone which we followed all the way to its confluence with the River Parrett at Burrow Bridge. Cygnet rings congregated on the opposite bank under grey skies with a helpful south-westerly wind. Ancient tales appeared around the levels where King Arthur did naughty things to invading Scandinavian monarchs for all the right reasons at the time. A clump (part of the ancient Althelney Abbey?) appeared. This was the monastery that dwindled (was altered?) to a church. The clumpy hill-lark became a recurring theme in Somerset as later that day we could see the hills at Street and Glastonbury. Jesus, no one at the inn of Burrowbridge, or of Othery but the bakery was heaven sent. A sumptuous lunch of the big breakfast kind then we left carrying sausage rolls for Moidie (there was no other shop so no dog food), and a lardy cake for us. The A361 was a trudge against the traffic for 4 miles, then lumpy land for 3 miles. Who put the word 'level' in Somerset Levels? Blame the moles. My ankles did. A mile of road, then a drover's track which was actually laid with tarmac. Here, we had the first of two sightings of pronting fallow deer in their spring-spring mode. So much so, we thought they were kangaroos. A farmer had 'lost' a public footpath, adding an unwanted mile for us, but we were in good form (apart from Cathy's cold that made her sound rather sexy) so the plod over the Polden Hills was a fitting finale. Fully laden over 17 miles, our longest yet. Off to The Pike and Musket in Walton, a suburb of Street, for a veggie curry and a word with the gaffer about his dog policy. Hey, were there ghosts on the campsite? Moidie was spooked by our campsite pitch. Eerie!

## Day 15 Sat 02 April From Walton Nr Street to Old Down, near Midsomer Norton 17 miles

A couple of subjects need to be mentioned. Firstly, my shorts: I have employed a shorts-only policy, myself. This has developed a short-coming, if you pardon the pun, since the mighty nettle has begun to grow. Wearing my socks long makes me look an even bigger Wally and now the nettles out-reach those, too. My only consolation is the old wives' tale that the stings stave off arthritis. Well the way my ankle feels, I better go bare footing. My shorts were also too big for me, now, on account of walking off some good living. The trimmer me has necessitated a belt but as we never see a shop, bailer twine has sufficed. Yellow bailer twine. Rather fetching, in a Compo sort of way. The other subject is people, or rather their attitudes. Cornish people have top marks so far with time, politeness and general courtesy. Devonians were close to the same mark. Therefore, it has been with some dismay that, generally, the Somerset set have been well short of that mark. There have been endearing exceptions but there have been some grumpy souls in 'the levels.' We can tell by the on-coming traffic, shop-keeper discussions, 'Good Mornings' in the street and dog policies in pubs. We have clashed with land-owners, publicans, campsite owners, cyclists, pedestrians, motorists, farmers and shop assistants. Surely it's not us? Maybe Moidie's short fuse is infectious. Anyhow we walked through Walton into Street, the Quaker town that was tee total 30 years ago and the home of Clarks shoes. New roads or old maps? Either way, we discovered two bypasses, 12 miles apart that affected us. The first around Glastonbury who's Tor could be seen for most of our day and the second outside Wells where Cathedral and town nestled 'neath the Mendips. Long drover's lanes helped today although lack of grass underfoot brought damage to Cathy's tootsies, to add to a cold and a boil. We don't know if we were supposed to walk through the landscaped estate at Dinder but we got away with it. Architecture had taken another turn from Devon's rural cob farms to Cotswold-like stone masonry and Dinder, complete with a natural fountain, was a fabulous example. One final glance at Glastonbury Tor from 12 miles away, then the Mendips enveloped us in its lazy lanes. Then, a surprise call from Katie. They would pick us up from our intended stop, 4 miles south of Midsomer Norton. We galloped the last 2 miles along, firstly, Binegar Bottom and then the A37. We asked two girls, separately, if the pavement went all the way to the junction. They both needed to unplug ipod earphones before saying yes. Neither had a clue. The last one spoke to us only 50 yards from where the pavement ended, half a mile short of the junction. I was reminded of Evelyn Waugh's line: "I no longer speak to anyone under 40; it is just not worth the while". Katie and Siu, on the other hand, were worth their weight in golden light.

### Day 16 Sun 03 April From Old Down, near Midsomer Norton to Bitton, Avon 14 miles

Their sweetness continued into breakfast and taxi work to our re-starting point. Without our rucksacks, we light-footed it into the more gentle hills around Midsomer Norton. The only severe slope was the slagheap from coal mining around Radford. It was close by this lump that the grey skies opened for a deluge. Luckily a hotel was ahead, advertising a bar. We had no waterproof trousers with us, so our legs got soaked as the entrance evaded us. Just to make sure we were drenched, I insisted we went right round the building to find an open bar that did not exist. We dripped over the sofa as the inefficient owner served lovely coffee and two Elizabeth Shaw mint crisps. Cathy thought this was two each, I kept to a diet. Back out on our generally uneventful walk, we talked to Moidie despite her being left back in Bristol. With Bath on our right and Bristol on our left, the skies blackened and, miraculously The Wheatsheaf appeared in the middle of nowhere. It poured. Cider helped the strides away from the Mothers' Day parties and over the southern ridge of the Avon valley, leaving Somerset behind us. The walk ended in differing circumstances. From Saltford, on the floor of the valley, the riverside opened up from the edge of a quintessential English village down to the water meadows. Then the big downer: we could not cross The Avon at Swinford. We recalled Cathy's phone call to the pub on the opposite bank. In March we asked "Can we cross at the weir?" "Yes." "Are you sure?" (I chastised Cathy for being pushy at the time) "Yes". They lied. Or they were ignorant. Or both. Take your choice. I swore all the extra 2 miles to Bitton.

## Day 17 Mon 04 April From Bitton, Avon to Horton Nr Chipping Sodbury 10.5 miles

It was Cathy's turn to swear, today. A deeply ploughed field, where the Monarch's Way should have been, caused it. There was no edge to the field and no sniff of a reinstated path. Oh, she did swear. I just loaded my imaginary shotgun. Three extra miles, it cost us, and an end to a lovely morning's walk up the Golden Valley, through Wicks, along streams on soft grass footpaths that form the Monarch's Way up to the M4. Not always in sunshine, the Cotswold influence was evident in the ridge topography and village architecture. A fine taste of a special place in England. The wind helped us to eventually to make Chipping Sodbury in time for the last lunch served at the tea room. Ah, kippers. The town had more of the Cotswold charm. It was where everyone over 70 must wear cream. We left at 4pm for the last 2 ½ miles across an adorable common, used for grazing, into

Horton where Cathy spat out the last of her feathers before Siu did the kind ferrying.

## Day 18 Tue 05 April From Horton Nr Chipping Sodbury to Wooton Under Edge 7 miles

Rain was anticipated today and we wanted Katie to walk some way with us tomorrow. Maybe, just maybe, we would be happy for an easy day and a bit of an afternoon snooze. I never got the latter but Cathy snores as I write. It was a frog-march of 7 miles to Wotton Under The Edge. We only got light drizzle, but it gave the full waterproofs some exercise. The first wild bluebells were out and most trees are in junior leaf stages. This was hilly enough for our battered bodies and the rest with a newspaper was a luxury. Thanks to Siu again for being our taxi.

## Day 19 Wed  06 April From Wooton Under Edge to Stroud 13 miles

The warmest day of the year and Katie joined us for the first 4 miles from Wotten to Dursley, hills and all. The Cotswolds had glorious sunshine to show off its shoulders and give us vistas across the full tide Severn, over the Welsh ridges to the Black mountains nudging above. To the north we had the Malvern Hills providing a focus throughout the time we were in the open or had not got our nose in a steep, long slope. We began on lanes up and down wooded hills, then on footpaths through such woodland with the calls of fresh warblers settling into their summer homes. Celandine still lined the banks while bluebells, swallows and tree leaves all emerged for their first look at this year's British sunshine. Blackcaps seem to be the latest invader in high numbers with our brimstone and peacock butterflies making fluttering appearances. The man heralded as the translator of the Bible into English, Mr. Tyndall (William) was celebrated by a high obelisk. In his time he was heralded enough to be burnt at the stake for his heresy. Nicer things happened to us, although waving good-bye to Katie and Moidie on the 311 bus from

Dursley was not one of them (both lovelies are pictured). The decision to leave Moidie behind in her second home was the correct one. A stiff shoulder and a lack of natural water supply influenced us but above all she loves her surrogate family. Softer footpaths and flat recycled train-tracks eased our way into the valley town of Stroud, a little further on than planned. The ankles needed a rest so we hit a welcome B&B in a pub, The Clothier Arms.

## Day 20 Thu   07 April From Stroud to Seven Springs Nr Cheltenham 13.5 miles

Stroud has streams. Even, big, busy towns give beautiful views when they have waterways and the burgeoning sun at 9 am gave a picture of tranquillity in a commuter-driven world. The view from the northern peak of Folly Lane showed Stroud nestling in a crown of rural hills. No wonder the town has so many waterways with such a catchment profile. We had hauled our fully-breakfasted stomachs up the mile long escarpment in warm sunshine. The sound of business had soon been lost to the warbling of blackcaps. The lane quickly lost its tarmac on the edge of the woodland. The last of the lane was lined with white daffodils which had an aesthetic appeal as the direction arched round bends.

There were to be no more towns today. The rural settings were a blessing especially on some of the B road sections. The Foresters Ash Inn served us orange and lemonade at 11 as news came texting through that Sturmers would be at the Royal George Hotel in Birdlip at 1-30. Buzzards and a cronking raven flew by and so had the miles. We had done 9 ½ miles by Birdlip, so a good lunch was in order. Colin, Jan and `mum' had tales of Scotland to swop as well as encouragement to give. Not only was it lovely to see them, but we hung on until 4pm watching the Aintree race meeting where Sam Twiston-Davies at 16 won the Foxhunters Chase. More mottled skies covered our tracks to Leckhampton Hill where lads were trying to rescue an old Range Rover that attempted to drive over one ridge too many. They gave us the name of The Hungry Horse pub at Severn Springs, just south of Cheltenham, so we pitched in its car park only yards from the noisy convergence of several main roads. We still ask ourselves 'Why?'.

## Day 21 Fri 08 April From Seven Springs Nr Cheltenham to Winchcombe 12 miles

An even warmer day, today. Suzie's breakfast van not only provided bacon baps for bleary eyed campers. We also got directions to the source of The Thames (as well as the source of the tomato, mustard and mayonnaise if we wanted it). Hence the "Severn Springs". Duly educated, we left the noisy traffic that had kept me awake to attack the hills. More than any day so far, it was mainly footpaths all the way and predominantly The Cotswold Way. "The futile hill" scenario played its part once again as we climbed towards the north-facing escarpment of Cleeve Hill, our highest point to date. We were very slow. Blame lasts night's traffic, severe contours, the nattering tea-lady in the woods, passing conversations, a wounded adder or wonderful, wonderful views. We were very slow. My ankles, Cathy's fears (for her and me) and general leg weariness added to the list of excuses but it was probably all the best because it was probably our finest to date. Plotting our way over the grass haven of Cleeve Common, avoiding golf balls where necessary, we eventually found the final spur of land dropping 1,000 feet over 3 miles into Winchcombe. I chatted to Lindsey and Mike West outside the Co-op who swiftly offered their front garden for the tent, so there we went. It was opposite the rear car park to the Corner Cupboard pub where we had watched The Topham Chase in the bar (not in the bar, but at Aintree). Always Waining won, not a topical name. It was there that I entertained the locals by tripping down the steps as they wished us a safe journey. The tent came under attack. We were sitting on the garden bench, fearful that the West's dog `Nuts' would befit his name and tear our beloved Vaude to shreds, when the local tomcat came to spray the whole inside, I clouted it but all it did was to go around the other side of the tent for another bollock shake. The more I clouted, the more he spayed. I got wise, I left him alone. He was empty by then anyway. I dreamt in shades of cat's pee. Regular airings and wipe downs are attempting to cure the ills.

## Day 22 Sat 9 April From Winchcombe to Broadway
## 9.5 miles

Even hotter? Perhaps. Lindsey brought tea and would have provided breakfast but for our insistence on an early start (ish). It was 9am by the time Winchcombe saw our feet toddle to the quiche stall at the WI sale. Fresh fudge, too. All to be eaten on a hillside where only the lambs could see us. Blazing sun would have called on our split-day strategy but for the Grand National, so we only took easy breaks as we skimmed the classic Cotswold settlements of Stanway and Stanton where fine halls, parklands and trainer Smiley's horses abound. With grass underfoot again, we climbed more than we hoped but enjoyed much of the Cotwold Way as a consequence. Broadway was full of smart Welsh visitors with cream teas on their mind. The tourist information booked us into her own self-contained apartment at Hunter's Lodge, so Cathy was able to watch her £2 each way on 14/1 Ballabrigs win the National and put cash in the coffers.

## Day 23 Sun 10 April From Broadway to Aston Cantlow
## 17 miles

Slept like dormice. The long rest sure helps, but so did the `Cushnsteps' insoles Cathy insisted on buying with her winnings. Hunter's Lodge breakfast in the main house was quintessential Cotswolds with tales of Jodami's Gold Cop celebrations with Mark Dwyer taking over our host restaurant 'til 4am. Sunny but the morning chill allowed us a 3mph pace over tranquil lanes until the Sunday Lunch Brigade broke ranks. In general, the flashier the car, the less courteous the driver. Obesity was set on the same correlation. But, most were fine, especially bikers. Blackthorn was going over and hawthorn was in full leaf. Whitethroats and orange tip butterflies formed an avenue for us, as did the horse chestnuts into Bidford On Avon, conquering all before them. Lunch on the Avon's banks allowed us to take in the fact that we had made it to Warwickshire. Their hospitality was exemplified by Anne and Brian Page who had driven by us that morning and called us in for afternoon tea with honey and ginger cake. Their smiles lightened our feet. Then a little old lady Helen shuffled up in carpet slippers with a toy collie. "Some say I walk Lucky too far," she said. We sided with her, knowing how dogs love a stroll. We believed she might make it to the cross-roads, a mile away. She pressed on much further than that. We observed several panoramic views with her on the succession of minor summits before asking her "How far will you go today?"

"Only to Alchester and back", she said softly. That worked out at 10 miles. Such a tiny old lady, but such a might. A blessed meeting to a worthy fellow walker. We celebrated seeing our first cowslips as we parted. Through Ardens Grafton, Temple Grafton, Haselor (Hogan's Cider home) and into a charitable camp site at Aston Cantlow. Hens, ducks and geese came calling. I've always been good with the birds. Not a bad day at all. Only fell over once!

## Day 24 Mon 11 April From Aston Cantlow to Knowle, near Solihull       11 miles

It transpired that Cathy thought Helen was as mad as a fish because Cathy had heard Helen say "I had a little drink last week and never knew what I did for 4 days." Sweet thing. We woke around 7 am this morning, by which time most things with wings sounded like they were shagging. A free pot of tea from the nice lady of Island Meadow Campsite joined our banana and cheese wraps for breakfast as hens congregated for crumbs. The last of the black timbered white houses were behind us before we noticed the architectural change. A few miles later we joined the Stratford Upon Avon Canal and only a few more before we left it to climb some pointless hills. Well, Cathy wanted to see gardens again. She is now clear of colds, blisters, boils and coughs although the pain in the neck is still married to her. Flowering rape seed created a yellow swathe on the landscape and gardener's hyacinths provided the perfumed remedy. Back on the Stratford Upon Avon Canal at the Fleur De Lys, near Finwood, but only after pies with lots of gravy. The canal had too many locks to make it fun for the holiday makers. No barges overtook our dawdle. Nor did the most enormous bum we had seen to date. We spent 2 miles discussing how she wiped it. Cathy broke into song, mainly silly ones. Did 10 lords go a'leaping? A dead deer floated by, then we switched canals, over to the Grand Union. True, it was grander, but hardly a barge moving. We stopped at the Black Boy pub for some local knowledge only to find that there wasn't any. 400 yards on was a pub they failed to mention: The Heron's Rest. Ross, the gaffer, let us camp for free. Do you fancy a pint? Ross even donated our meal for free. A chilly night with ice in the shade.

## Day 25 Tue 12 April From Knowle, near Solihull to Nether Whiteacre    15 miles

Not that I noticed. Snug as a hog in a snog, me. Not only were we allowed to use the loos, but Lindsey invited us to have breakfast and take some fruit for the journey. The smell of good coffee was not denied. Back onto the canal we found further evidence of Brummie bon ami as we scaled the 7? locks of Knowle's Ladder. The north-westerly wind kept the heat of the sun at bay and only helped us once we took to the road east to Eastcote and onto Hampton in Arden, where schoolboy humour broke out at the word Hampton. Here, too, we were offered tea at Liz and Simon's house where the alarm had been set off by the house rabbit. I put out a warren for its arrest. Walking well, we were, helped by a shorter day yesterday. We found a short cut before Meridan (the centre of England by some measurement) that entailed a harrowing experience through an archery centre before climbing fences, dragging rucksacks through hedges and dodging dual-carriageway traffic on the A45/M42 interchange. The road to Maxstoke was labelled with a sign that read "Dogging". We only saw a lone man in a transit van (it wasn't rocking), so the mysteries of this phenomenon still befuddle us. We passed the Forest of Arden Hotel, scene of a glorious company bash in 2004, then compared out tent to the Jacuzzi-in-the-room luxury of those affluent days in industry. The Plough at Stustoke (I'm not making these up) had the same amount of grass as local information. The gaffer had not heard of Solihull, 8 miles away! Beginning to register on the knackered scale, we forced 2 more miles on the Centenary Way to Whiteacre Heath where the two pubs were our bankers. "You don't want them", said Brummy Big Andy, "Walk an extra mile to my local pub, they'll treat you right", as he stuffed ice lollies in our hands at the shop. So, off to The Gate at Nowhere City (OK, I made that one up, it was at Nether Whiteacre - still not sure are you?) Two steaks, three pints and heaps of bollocks talked with the lovable Big Andy. The pints were the locally brewed Marston's Pedigree (we walked through Marston the next day). The bollocks included "Nether Whiteacre is the highest place in Warwickshire at 900ft. The OS says it's only 330 ft and three miles away it's 500 ft. As for the gravitational pull of the nearest moon for 5,000 years splitting the world apart causing tsunamis, well let me float with those fairies. Lovely pub sign: One tequila, two tequilas, three tequilas, FLOOR! Big Andy, 54, was a fun man.

## Day 26 Wed  13 April From Nether Whiteacre to Hopwas 10 miles

Back on track under dark clouds, we decided, or rather our bodies convinced us, to have a shorter walk this day. Pavement soon turned towpath where we walked past `Contentment', a barge we saw many times on the Birmingham Canal into Tamworth. The two chaps, father and 30 year-old son maybe, at the rear were the most sullen silent type we had ever met. Cathy teased them as often as she could by asking annoyingly happy questions. They were on a week's holiday. It seemed more like a prison sentence. We strode purposefully into Tamworth. A reed warbler, a muntjac deer and the first hawthorn blossom made appearances on the canal bank. But Tamworth was a pig. Well, Blacks store was good. Maps, socks and our first meeting with somebody who had walked End to End. He did it from John O'Groat's in 30 days fully supported for Help The Heroes, so he route- marched the roads and could not advise us on the Southern Uplands quandary, but he was great to talk with. We even got his staff discount. Back to the sty: the Tourist Information Office had closed down. The £29 room advertised at the Premier Inn was £77-95. Pubs and hotels in a zigzag path they sent us on were all full. The new Tourist Information did not give information to tourists but could list the places that pay to advertise there. I made that observation. The lady insisted their world was perfect. They weren't allowed to tell me about the pub on the A51 roundabout that they knew of and might have helped. So I suggested a relaunch as "Withholding Tourist Information." A donated watch battery by Marie at Christopher's Jewellers and lunch at the A51 pub helped us to calm down. In the end the 118118 trail led us to a B&B out of town on the banks of the River Tame. The four-poster bed, sumptuous bath, glorious views and pampering were everything we needed. I'm not too sure if we will leave Hopwas (still not making it up).

## Day 27 Thu   14 April From Hopwas to Tatenhill 13 miles

A second bath, just to make sure. The black pudding with the grand breakfast confirmed we were in Staffordshire. It was then the turn of the Coventry Canal to give us a spring towpath where three mallard chicks were paraded as the first of the season. A father of twin 4 year-old boys proved barge owners who live the canal life are generally better folk than the one week wonders we see tight lipped and moribund. He was a senior school teacher allowing his kids to absorb life's lessons from nature, so he loved the news of the first chicks down the bank for his lads to see. Lunch in Alrewas only needed to be pork scratchings at the packed George and Dragon. Great to see no tables available. Good cheap pub grub had filled the place. Along the Trent we went, past the Memorial National Arboretum to pay our respects to our fallen military, then onto Burton Under Needwood after being held up by a man venting his spleen over the awful Yankee takeover of Burton Brewery where he will retire from shortly and join us walking if his knee holds out. Ladies chatted to us in Barton, one of whom walked wild over the Great Glen Way this week and had a ball. Then rural scenery again round the Dunstan Estate and onto Tattenhill's Horseshoe pub where Mrs Lipp gave us a pitch when four other pubs ahead were unable to. Roast beef dinner and Bread and butter pudding all for £5-95 and locals talking over life's riches led us to bed by the ducks and miniature goats. It was these that woke us amid the fine dawn chorus, shortly before the gaffer gave us morning tea.

## Day 28 Fri 15 April From Tatenhill to Osmarston 16 miles

With a light breeze and higher cloud we set off at a fair pace until a crab and prawn baguette in Tutbury weighed us down. We realised that what we eat affects the way we walk. Perhaps I should chew rocket fuel. Crossing the free flowing River Dove into Derbyshire made us think we weren't as free flowing as we should be. We had a Fanta to zap us up at Hatton. The crab was still winning. On the edge of the next hamlet we collapsed for a 40 minute sleep. That seemed to shuffle the shellfish (at a pinch) The sun blasted us for half an hour then was gone for the day, smothered by dark clouds that never threw the rain they threatened. It dulled the view of leafy but level lands as we swopped lanes for the grassy bridleways. Saying we were walking The Bonnie Prince Charlie Way may sound effeminate, so I talked low and manly just in case. Good job, because I had to look my best before slipping into Shirley. Pulling out again was a disappointment as the pub was shut and probably not good for camping, Bonny or not. Sagging as the miles were taking a toll, we met with a mother and daughter who fairly galloped with us down and up through a large estate before arriving in the neat village of Osmaston. We found this was still estate owned but the landlord let us pitch in the family playpen overlooking the rural setting under the gentle chimes from the local church. 16 miles began to feel quite a long way for the day. Paul and Tina with soccer-mad Alex and Lee (keep training with the left peg, lads) entertained us with real English pub fare without sparing the fresh veg. Then toast and tea greeted us in the morning.

## Day 29 Sat 16 April From Osmarston to Biggin 13 miles

A bright dawn soon mottled over to be an overcast day: fine for walking. Cathy had developed a headache with the help of only one grouse, Famous though it was. This got worse by late afternoon. Ashbourne did not help: it was a town. Even worse: it had a Sainsbury's. This failed to offer either a cafe, an envelope or a sun-protection stick. Oh, but we gave it some stick. It was in a lot of trouble. Its sandwiches spent so much effort telling us how healthy they were that they forgot to provide any taste. So, Mr & Mrs Annoyed-With-Towns-And-Sainsbury's marched off for the Tissington Trail. This gave us a complete sea-change of topography (if that is possible). These large limestone hills signalled the beginning of our country's backbone: The Pennines and we were at the start of The (Alan Jackson's) Pennine Bridleway. Our dear pal was the chartered surveyor who negotiated the rights of way for this national trail, so we felt pretty darn good to be stamping all over his work. This was deep-cut landscape where valleys cut too deep for us to see the full extent of the water-erosion. Dove Dale, the most visited of them all, ran close by this recycled railway track which forms part of Route 68, The Pennine Cycle Path. Do I tell the "A1 walks into a bar" joke? No? Be thankful.

Over the first hour 50 Muslim schoolgirls of 14 years old cycled the slight downhill line from 13 miles away, some cycling for the very first time, they told us. It was fun for them until they had to turn round to cycle the same distance uphill. Some will still be there now. Our own world was not perfect either. My rucksack's squeak had reached annoying proportions given Cathy's headache. The annoyance gave rise to a complete overhaul of the complex "bioflex" system, a matrix of ratchets, rods and levers that would have scared a quantum mechanic. If I had studied origami and black-belt Meccano sets, it would have been a synch. As it was, I relied upon good luck and plenty of swearing. It seemed I got away with it. The only down side: great tits no longer sing back to me.

A Roger joined us for a few miles... I know: "Roger The walker". ... then a lady who saw us in Tamworth saw us again pitching our tent at 4.30 at The Waterloo Inn's campsite. Tea and cake on our arrival was our prize from her.

It is worth mentioning accents now as we have travelled over many regional boundaries. The easy-paced Cornish tongue drifted into gentle Devon drawl before the cider-twangs of Somerset gave the base and bass of the Bristol burr and the ensuing Cotswold country tones. Harsher sounds developed around Birmingham to a point where everyone had their nose bunged up, yet it soon added a northern weight early in Staffordshire. So now, in Derbyshire we have lost the Brummie influence altogether. Therefore, this totally comprehensive Dialectology Dissertation concludes that local accents do not change in steps but evolve by bending round corners. Goodnight.

## Day 30 Sun 17 April From Biggin to Peak Forest, Derbyshire     16.5 miles

Someone kill that cockerel. We could say a cock gets one up early... Back to The Tissington Trail via the grassy expanses around Heathcote where the morning Peak landscape looked a picture of true England. Our early start had got the jump on the crowds, so peace reigned for the 5 miles to Parsley Hay, the summit of the track where the bacon baps lived. The tent came out for a drying session while we watched people pretending to be cyclists. Real ones never need to pose. Sunday morning peddlers with everything hired, especially the florescent bits, have to.

The next section opened up, showing the range of limestone hills and the many sink holes within them. No rubber plugs in sight. One man, alone on a remote raised bank had cycled 5 hours from Leicestershire, slept overnight to watch the early peregrine falcons and would leave before it got busy.

The Tissington Trail ended but Al's Bridleway kept heading for the Pennines proper by taking us to their western edge. We found a massive drop that was Chee Dale, a deep-cut valley holding the SSSI (Site of Special Scientific Interest) area of the River Wye (not the Welsh one). Why Oh why. What a canyon. The ankles did not like it, but the eyes and heart had a ball. This was the sharpest down-and-up to date, under sharp cliffs of rock a couple of hundred feet high. The zigzag up and out skirted Buxton's Old Moor Lime quarry, a lunar landscape, in stark contrast to the massive green blocks of land that opened in front of us. The days walk was one of our best, aided by the target of the B&B at Peak Forest which we booked by phone en route once we realised the legs were working well enough for the 16 mile tramp. Still, there was a sting in the tail. A stone on the road found itself under my left ankle for the fall No. 3, so we both struggled for the final mile. That bed better be worth it. Once there, we realised it wasn't perfect. I also realised that I had been wearing a coin in my sock, so a perfect 20p piece bruise developed. If you had wanted to see what the Queen looked like when she is mature... that was the moment. Noisy kids in the bar, on the bar, over the chairs, table and top, generally got the Cathy teacher treatment. Their parents had no control, but Cathy did. Job done. They even cried. Job *very* well done.

## Day 31 Mon   18 April From Peak Forest, Derbyshire to Charlesworth, Nr Glossop 15 miles

We sleep worse in a bed than we do in our tent. Confirmed. Today, we walked in the Pennines proper, High Peak, they call it. It was the Pennines for sure, ask my feet. The views were stunningly vast. We had run away from Kinder, the monster mound to our east, but the route of the Pennine Bridleway took us up and down sharply several times. The delight of the day was the curlew. Old bent-nose piped us over the moorland passes all day. Golden plovers, lapwings, meadow pipits and a wheatear also entertained us in a land bereft of humans and densely populated by silence. A south easterly eased our way, gusting a soil storm of dust at 1,000ft. Coffee at The George Hotel in the steep sided Hayfield barely fuelled us for the ascent of the Giggle-Gaggle footpath. Grouse scattered in the heather on our first day among bilberries, then a road slog into Charlesworth.  How far down? The Grey Mare (finest chips) was full of Uncle Tom Cobbley and all. It was Don Booth who volunteered a lawn for our pitch. "The wife might kill me, but don't worry." Well Dianne did not kill Don as we were made to feel very welcome. Like many ladies, though, she wanted time to tidy up the bathroom before we went to the loo.

## Day 32 Tue 19 April From Charlesworth, Nr Glossop to Diggle 15.5 miles

One calendar month and still going. One very small blister each early on gives a rave reference for our Inov8 shoes and proof that our feet can take more than our ankles. Incredibly, there was another half mile further down into Charlesworth, as the plummet line went. Then straight back up at Broadbottom. An interesting name. I would not mind living in Lower Broadbottom but not Upper Broadbottom.

Therein, so to speak, was the Sunflower Sandwich Bar where Dave and Karen made the world's best bacon and egg mega-roll. What Karen's long lost brother in America will make of our photo, God knows. So, up and down through Mottram where Lowry's statue was sat on a bench near his final home of 20 years. Over the col, Stalybridge gave us a mile long slope tobogganists would die for. This got us to the Huddersfield small gauge canal, famous for the Standedge Tunnel where barge men used to "walk" the ceiling for three miles under the Pennines. That's where we ended but not before meeting the local thicko. He appeared along the towpath in the blazing sunshine shortly after we had met a cyclist who had lost his wife due to facebook then he had found God. Thicko wore only pantaloon shorts and trainers. Neither was tasteful but they were in keeping with his bull-headedness, beer belly and dentistry. He smiled (with gaps) as he, his sunken eyed wife and seven kids bundled towards us. "Ehh-oop! Where thee goooin'?" He lisped as only one with the front six teeth missing can lisp. Any teeth left were mere pegs on the endangered list. We showed him the sign and told him in case he could not read. "Land's End?" (No clue) He said, "Where's that?"
"Cornwall." ... Still no clue.
"Nice pub juusst oop there," He pointed to the next bend, "You'll need tha'." His stomach nearly swotted one bairn into the canal as he turned and waddled into our folklore.
A good canal walk saw us rise without noticing it. From Uppermill it became a popular tourist trip and the locks were more frequent until Diggle where the tunnel started. "Where's Fred" was filming for Granada TV. He chatted long enough for us to realise what a bore he was. A fact reconfirmed when he caught us at The Diggle Hotel as we pitched our tent on the car park's two blades of grass. Fresh lamb and leek pie made me forget even my ankle pain before tucking into the cheese and biscuits. We fell to sleep listening to trains entering the tunnel.

## Day 33 Wed 20 April From Diggle to Walsden, West Yorks. 17 miles

Off at 8, straight up, west of the Standedge Ridge, and then straight down to the first of a series of reservoirs (all low to the brim). Ankles hurt, so I need mothering. Cathy did the job by telling me where the edges and loose rocks were. The north easterly wind bit until mid afternoon but the sun kept the temperatures high enough for us to fear moor fires. We found the worst-kept bridleway at Denshaw, spoiled by a moaning farmer who blamed Chernobyl for his divorce. It looked like everything he touched fell apart. A high pub`s tearoom was more of a champagne-room; weird on top of a moor to find haute cuisine. Nice soup, though. It was a big moment when we saw and crossed the M62. Putting it to the south felt good. Hollingworth Lake was the honey-pot of the area, packed with townies looking to get sunburnt. The pub was full of chip lovers, hundredweights of them. Reinforce that decking, Gaffer! Local advice continued to prove that people give you the answer they think you want rather than the truth. We even begun to appreciate those who had no idea what goes on in their region, but admitted it, rather than the sort who sent us on wild goose chases for paths, directions and several B&B's that failed to exist. Yet happiness was with so many folk who spoke to us. One fisherman on the Rochdale Canal (having used a ladder to drop down from his garden to be bank-side) got his wife to give us magnum ice lollies from their freezer. That was at Summit where they boast the highest broad lock in the country as the watershed took effect on the Lancashire/West Yorkshire boundary. Sweltering heat, we beat a mournful pace to the only B&B in Walsden: The Cross Keys. On a busy road but, with no opportunity to pitch a tent: a last resort. Oddly, having gone through the town on our search the pub was on the canal we were advised to leave. Locals, eh?

## Day 34 Thu 21 April From Walsden to Widdop Edge, outside Hebden Bridge 11 miles

If you brought a barge, what would you call it? We played this game and came up with "Oops!" Leaving the Cross Keys was no hardship. Even the milk portions in our room had dried to mouldy cheese inside their small plastic pots. Right, we said, we will only do a little walk. Hebden Bridge, that's only 6 miles. Well, we decided to put a hill or four further behind us than that. The walk for me stopped after only four paces. Still getting the rust out of my ankles I watched my left ankle so carefully on the cobbles leading from the pub that my right ankle found a rat hole and over I went. No real harm done, we wandered under clear skies and meagre wind to Hebden Bridge nestling at a meeting point of three mighty hills. A picnic lunch on the canal bank was eagerly watched by a pair of canada geese. On the other bank, a heron sought his own lunch. The hill out of town was described as a "crampon" hill, passing through the small laned village of Heptonstall clinging to the side of said hill. Sylvia Plath was buried there, close to where her husband, poet laureate Ted Hughes was born. A final glorious valley at Hardcastle Crags proved once again that Cathy's uphill thrust exceeded mine today by about three fold. My legs could be called free-fold. Then on top of a remote hill was our B&B: the Pack Horse Inn, a stable-edged premise providing a stop for riders on the Pennine Bridleway (Alan Jackson's PBW). Two B&B's in a row? Well the last one was rubbish and this one was strategically placed as the last food to get us to the next stop without starting with a "crampon hill".

## Day 35 Fri 22 April From Widdop Edge, outside Hebden Bridge to Earby YHA 13.75 miles

We found out the stables were for their own horses, some of which were National Hunt horses owned by them (as Widdop Wanderers) and put on their grass out of season. Talk of Cheltenham and their Royal Emperor in the 2004 Gold Cup carried us through breakfast. It had been our remotest B&B with only the hills for neighbours and birdsong rather than car noise from our open bedroom window. The hazy sun of dawn kept the views mystical for most of the morning. Red grouse competed with curlew for air time in terms of sound while meadow pipits even beat the many wheatears for flying time, drawing us from their nest-sites. The paths across the moor were our main routes today including the Bronte Way close to Witkins (the inspiration for Wuthering Heights) and the Pendle Way (this one marked with a witch on a broomstick). It was very hot, so an ice cream milk shake in Trawden was a welcome treat. We met some nice walkers on the way although the 25 young folk (aged 20 to 30) walking to the Pack Horse Inn from 4 miles away probably only made the first 3 of them. Farmers were playing games with bridleways again. This time round Kelbrook, where a few swear words and a dismantling of a shackle made us feel better. Then came the weak, yellow-livered, snobby-gobbed Youth Hostel man who failed every test of decency. His failures were all our fault despite us ringing ahead and him failing to ring us back. So no tent there. Up yours you sad, lonely (and we can see why) uncharitable snooty dog-brain. So we went to the local green tucked behind some cottages. Free of Hitler.

## Day 36 Sat 23 April From Earby YHA to Airton 11.25 miles

Hail St George. The sound of gentle waterfalls held us asleep for over 9 hours so the earliest sounds I recalled were the shepherd marshalling his dogs way up on the distant hills. Belly Buster Baps contain more protein than anybody on my medication should see in a week but, hell I'm walking it off. The jolly Samaritans Pat and Alan Jackson (yep, that's them in the next picture) found us mid-mouthful. Then Alan drove off to Gargrave and walked back along the Pennine Way to meet us, with Pat walking over the moorland from Earby, chatting furiously as we went. The cycle cafe as everyone knows it provided a nibble for the Jacksons but the Beard Bellies were still busting, so a drink sufficed. Then Alan drove to Airton (where a formula one driver can be found in the centre?) and repeated the trekking back routine, but this time Cathy, Pat and I lost the Pennine Way. All down to that furious chatting malarkey. Cathy went up one hill; I tried another, by which time Alan had travelled much further than half way with only lime sweets as company. From this sunny summit we dropped to the River Aire, aptly named as it had hardly any water in it. Many gates and stiles later, we had swopped tales and reduced Alan's lime sweets to single figures. By the time the hillside primroses heralded us to the grey stone bridge outside Airton, Cathy and I felt good for a few more miles after a late lunch. However, by the time we had walked 200 yards to the farmyard cafe we had booked into the gorgeous looking B&B house next door. Lovely cakes and farm shop classic nosh. Sod the extra miles!

## Day 37 Sun 24 April From Airtonto
## Outside Horton -in-Ribblesdale 12 miles

Lovely breakfast to match the weather, then off early enough to avoid the Easter traffic. The low car count on the minor roads we used meant we need not have bothered. There were no settlements between Airton and Settle, so moorland views and piping curlews kept us happy as we rose sharply by steady progression. The limestone scars around Malham could be seen through a col prior to Ingelborough and Penyghent. These two dominated the valley of Ribblesdale, on either side as the day progressed. It was 6 miles to our pancakes in Settle, the last half mile of which was spent leaning back so our rucksacks did not tip us into a rolling ball down the steep gradient. Cyclists went like bullets past us at 40 mph. Once on the river bank path, the hordes of tourists were lost, all stuck to the town's honey-pot centre. Seven miles further on was Horton in Ribblesdale where we found Mr. Sutcliffe's Cragghill farm for a night's pitch. A bit short of food, so the lambs look like dinner. I failed to catch any of Bo Peep's darlings so we had to make do with dry cheese and a cheese and onion crisp bap (half each).

## Day 38 Mon 25 April From Outside Horton -in- Ribblesdale to Cowdub, Dentdale, Cumbria 12.5 miles

Our stomachs drove us for the mile into Horton as soon as the tent dried in the northerly wind that was to be in our faces all day. The sun was only working part time and left work entirely by 2pm. It shone on the Ribble by the rustic campsite and overheated us on the steep inclines out of the valley along The Ribble Way on our disjointed route to The Dales Way over miles of barely interrupted moorland. We were always heading east of Ribblehead but always close enough for us to get grand views of our country's largest viaduct. Our path out from Ribblesdale's birth was a steep one. So much so I need to confess to three refusals, no falls but two submissions. Cathy thundered on and my only chances of catching her up were stiles where she crossed like the unoiled Tin Man. Once across the watershed, the red grouse serenaded us onto the small road down under the smaller viaduct of Dentdale (yet still mighty) and alongside the limestone step waterfalls of the River Dent. Just 3 miles down the road was the expected Sportsman Inn and the unexpected farmer's campsite at Cowdub. Basic is all we need when the pub offers more than a dry cheese and onion crisp bap. (half each).

## Day 39 Tue 26 April From Cowdub, Dentdale, Cumbria to Howgill, Nr Sedburgh 12 miles

It was a windy night (nothing to do with Dent Aviator Ale). The north easterly wind was still biting as we packed up, maybe because we were still high in Dentdale, we thought at the time. Yet it kept its teeth all day although spasmodic sunshine played its part to even out the temperature. The wind was on our back, which was more than we can say for our rucksacks because Pat and Alan found us wandering early enough to repeat the ferrying-and-walk back routine of Saturday. Surprising, it was that they found us at all as phone contact was zero due to the help of BT maintenance "sorry for any delay" (the sign automatically displaced on the screen of the remote phone box). No wonder rural phones get rage wrecked. Anyway, the walk along the River Dent, into the adorable town of the same name and further along the river could have been the fiction of Beatrix Potter. Mike Harding (now the Dales Preservation Society's President) reckoned this was the most beautiful dale. Well if Peter Rabbit had skipped all the way in front of us, it would not have surprised me or my walking companion, Jemima Puddleduck. The high walls of moorland fells, the lush lowland meadows and the limestone layers of the river bed made this a stunning yet easy walk for us all. An up-and-over from Dentdale to the River Rawthey brought us face to face with the Howgills, large fells of almost mountainous imposition, cradling the classic grey-stone town of Sedburgh. Finding good cafes with the Jacksons has now reached professional status, so curried soup on the menu was hardly a shock. What was a shock was a Tourist Information Office which not only had tourist information but was willing to impart it! Hence, three miles further out on our intended path from Sedburgh, we arrived an hour after the Jackson two had dropped our heavy rucksacks at our remote B&B, down by the river. Now where's Jemima?

# Day 40 Wed  27 April From Howgill to Nowhere, 3 miles outside Orton    12.5 miles

Dorothy Parker (not the writer) was our host and fifth-generation owner of Thwaite Farm where lambing had benefited from this year's fine spring. We left this smiling lady for a day in the sun through the Howgills (those beautiful fells below).

The weather made this a glorious land despite the M6 in the distance. The story would have been different three weeks before when 48 hours of rain made the river Lune burst its banks and landslips of 100 years ago were rearranged into a 2011 design involving the manoeuvre of several tons of boulders. We saw the devastation as the lanes dropped to the river side footpath in woodland at the elbow on the young river. It was like crossing the floor of a Greek restaurant after the crockery joined the celebrations. There were sweet meadows too, with pied flycatchers, a Lune'y dipper (not skinny) and increasing numbers of swallows skimming the sheep pools for flies. The small settlement of Tebay boasts three railway carriages on just enough track to hold them in an old, disused railway siding. Just like my ankle joints in the morning, they can go neither forward or backwards. Tebays Old Schoolhouse is now a tearoom and B&B house of such homeliness that my life will be the poorer if I don't revisit its soups. Old Tebay took us close to the M6 and its services that looked a shabby show compared to the Schoolhouse just yards the other way. Then, 2 miles over a roller-coaster B road was Orton, the crossing point of this walk over The

Coast To Coast Walk. It was too hot for any goodies from the chocolate factory so sensible provisions were taken over the hill northwards to a remote wild camping spot where we had to shoo away the buzzard to pitch.

## Day 41 Thu 28 April From Nowhere, 3 miles outside Orton to Langwathby 15.5 miles

"There were frost ont pick-oop truck this morn'n," said a farmer. Our tent was 600 ft. higher up the fell than his farm, so we did well to cuddle our way through the night. An extra layer of clothes helped. I'd got up to tighten the guy-ropes at 5am when the eastern horizon wore scarlet lipstick. I was too asleep to feel anything but numb. We spent over 12 hours in bed, slept for 11, so we called it a good night. Young calves with doting mothers had been loaded into the next door field by the time we had risen and taken a breakfast of a scone and a pot of Happy Shopper yogurt. It's all we had. Our next food was five hours and 11 miles away because pubs and shops had closed down or were not to open until the evening. We found a lump or two of cinder toffee rolling in a rucksack pocket. It was like gold. The villages, although retail retarded, were beautiful. We followed a stream as it matured into the Lynvennit River which converged with Eden. The settlements each had features around its water course with village-green access to it at charming points. At Mauld Meaburn (yep, honest) there was a stone sculpture of a 6ft. high beehive in a sheepfold by Andrew Goldsmith and a more natural creation: a 13 ft. diameter, 500 million old sandstone lump as a millennium monument to prove how insignificant 2,000 years is in time. Cathy flagged as I dragged her to lunch at Temple Sowerby. I flagged as Cathy dragged me to Langwathby. We had pushed hard. So hard that we pushed some fun out of it. Yet along came Alan Jackson for the rendezvous and a welcome overnighter at Raughton Head. It can be as frosty as it likes tonight. We've got quilts.

## Day 42 Fri 29 April From Langwathby to Wethral 18 miles

Who ordered the confetti? It was a blustery day as the cherry blossom and the last of the blackthorn never stood a chance. How appropriate on the day William and Kate did a right Royal thing that we should be regularly showered with nature's confetti. The main street of Armathwaite had petal drifts that sloped from road to the top of the curb. Sweet. Yes it was windy as Alan dropped us off where we found him yesterday but this time, it was without our rucksacks. We strode lightly and mightily. There should have been a few fal-de-rees really but we were too interested in keeping warm. The sun did appear eventually but the wind always had the edge on a hazy day walking the river-terrace lanes on the west bank of the Eden. The Pennines diminished so much, that by the end of the day, they became The Penn-eights. The Calbeck Fells to the west were just as faded in the haze which concentrated the eye on the immediacy of the fast flowing, broad river and the banks of newly clothed trees. Flowering cow parsley flowers appeared so the cowslips will be hidden in a day or two. Soon the banks will be as dense as me. We walked well through Lazonby (no George) and into Armathwite for a drink where they tutted when we told them we did not want to eat. Pat's rolls were to blame. Oh, and the raspberry and cream turnovers. So snacks in the field gateways were lovely and sufficient on the hoof. With the backpacks at the Jacksons for the day, we aimed to get a bit of distance done. After 18 miles, we were pleased to see the cavalry to pick us up. Roast dinners, Katie and James as visitors, G&Ts and a bath........ do we really need to move on?

## Day 43 Sat 30 April From Wethral to Shankhill 15 miles

The Jackson Support Crew helped us to push onto the edge of the border. It was a lane walk for most of the way. Quiet ones, with just two crossings of A roads. The support vehicle held flasks and was used to fetch lunch for us near Fethergill. We crossed the Eden for the last time at Wetheral over a high footbridge beside the railway viaduct. Quite a send off. Irthington provided a tea break as the brisk south-easterly howled around the church yard under the clear sky that reigned (not rained) all day. We rose to the terrace of the River Irving as the bogs of the moorland began to appear in the poor lands of the borders. The Scottish hills lay ahead. Whether it was excitement or trepidation that lay within, Plod only knows.

## Day 44 Sun 1 May From Shankhill to Newcastleton, Scotland    12 miles

The amazing Jackson team had still one more task to perform. We did not even need to kidnap either a daughter or dog to force them; they carried our rucksacks into Scotland by driving on once they had dropped us off at Shankhill. The bright and breezy weather continued, though someone turned the wind velocity up a tad. There were no villages to go through today although Catlowdy pretended to be one. A farmer stopped us to make sure we were enjoying his views of the Pennines, Lakeland Mountains, Solway Estuary, Dumfries Hills and the undulations of the Borders. He accused us of being far too normal to be doing our walk but wished us luck. We could only imagine how bleak this area would be in winter, yet spring, however windblown, made it welcoming. We followed the River Liddel on its English bank for a few miles before crossing the border that follows its tributary, just before the old lime kiln on the hill above Newcastleton. There, in The Liddle Arms Hotel, we found the completed task of Alan and Pat. The long linear town was a designed settlement formed in the 18$^{th}$. Century, even before I was born. We pitched beside the Fire Station. Our neighbours were the convenient Public Conveniences.

## Day 45 Mon 2 May From Newcastleton, Scotland to 5 miles south of Hawick    16 miles

The wind died overnight. It was a pity it didn't take one noisy starling with it. However, we did hear our first cuckoo as we got up for breakfast at the Globe Hotel as prearranged for 8-15. So an early start set us on a road of 10 miles up a hill, then 10 miles down the other side to Hawick. We stopped 5 miles short of Hawick once we came across an unexpected B&B run by an ex-Harlow resident Kevin Webster. On our way over we followed one water, Hermitage Water, and came back down beside a more peaty burn. Two sandpipers at very close quarters and sand martins were highlights in the wildlife that gave us late celandine, primroses and violets as well as many orange- tip butterflies. The south easterly breeze picked up and got whipped around the bulges and funnels of smaller valleys. The views of the boarder land were vast. Almost as vast as the sighs of relief at that B&B sign.

## Day 46 Tue 3 May From 5 miles south of Hawick to Hawick 5 miles

A rest day. Kev and his wife were a double act from the old variety show days in the way he could not stop performing his life –history (I often anticipated a stiff cane and a boater to appear as a prelude to a soft shoe shuffle and a tap dance). His wife obediently smiled, chirping in with a Romford "I couldn't belieeeve it". At the end of breakfast, as Cathy was anxious to celebrate the effectiveness of yesterday's constipation tablet, Kev held her back with the "my Best Mate Got Murdered By His Own Son" routine. It was not a happy tale but hardly one to be interrupted with, "Sorry about your pal, Kev, but I need the loo." It was to be our rest day, but we weren't going to suffer that idiot Kev for two nights. To be fair, we had not decided then on our rest day. That came after I discovered I was knackered. A calf tear, buttock ache and sore feet: I could subscribe to anything. Cathy chipped in with a general plea for a break after six and a half weeks so, after we plodded 5 miles down the hill to Hawick, we booked into Hizzy's. The good weather made us feel guilty but self indulgence reigned supreme. Maps were reviewed and bought, my hair got a trim and I got sworn at by a mid-day drunk who was too Scottish for me to understand what was going on.

# Day 47 Wed 4 May From Hawick to 3 miles south of Melrose    13.5 miles

We have eaten too many fried breakfasts. Three biggies in a row got us sweating bacon fat. It was certainly hot enough once the overnight frost lost its hold. We left Franky and Hizzy to their booze and fags at 9-30, checked that the local bobby knew nothing about the local footpath just feet from where we stood, and then followed the Boarders Abbey's Way along the River Teviot for nearly 4 miles. The morning sun caught the fast flow as the footpath kept faith with the tree lined banks. A pair of goosanders sprung from the waters before we found the lanes out the valley. The undulations took us higher (then lower until going higher once more) to see the extensive hills all around us. To the far east we got to see The Cheviots which gave a mighty end to the Pennines.

We celebrated our decision not to flog ourselves over those heights. In front of us loomed the Eldon Hills, three massive lumps formed 450 million years ago. We ended up camping under the first of them at Faughhill (Brown Hill) farm courtesy of Dan and Nancy.

This was after a 90 minute lunch at the Jammy Coo in Lilliesleaf where the world's most scrumptious flapjacks are made. Burning under the sun, we had to walk a mile in and out and around the farm to find the farmer and our pitch, but, boy, what a spot (that's our flash Vaude lite Mk2, above).

Bad news on the shoes front: my fabulous innov8s have been worn down on the outside of both heels. They are not the sole things feeling over- the-heel.

## Day 48 Thu 5 May From 3 miles south of Melrose to Stow 14 miles

We are not getting any better at this. The day was fine, defying the forecasters' rain predictions. The quiet night gave us good sleep, so the walk over the hill and down the bouncy slope for a couple of miles into Melrose went well. It was steep into the Tweed Valley as we knew it would be. To get to the other side we crossed the Wire Bridge, but first we sought some new shoes. No shoe shops in Melrose (far too nice: an old market town with the famous Abbey), so rucksacks were left in the cafe while we took a bus to and from Gallashiels. A tedious event only bettered by an pointless attempt to get tourist information out of a tin with that label on it. So, to the Wire Bridge, a suspension job over the speedy Tweedy where a gillie aided a complete novice 40 something who had probably got the lesson as a gift from someone who wanted him to look like a tart. Success; job done. The north-shore path was part of The Southern Upland Way. The heron did not know this and nonchalantly departed as we walked by. We left the bank for the heron to return as soon as we could find the steepest road out of town (it wasn't actually a town or a road but you know what I mean). Boy it was hilly, and with all that faffing about in those town-things, we were getting tired. The packs were seeming heavier and the stops more frequent. I found the new shoes a dinger of an excuse. Cathy was only too happy to oblige. We found Meadow Field Golf Course (9 hole) and its cafe where a lady donated soup free of charge. From this oasis it went up, up, up, down, up, up down. You've got the idea. We kept telling the locals how brilliant we had found the boarders; how impressed we had been. Rubbish. We hated the hills. We lied. Well, the scenery was special, but only to look at as we were on our last legs coming over the final hill; we gave our lies to a local sort

who we asked for directions to our B&B when he stopped his 4 by 4. He informed us he was off there for a hair-cut. "Couldn't take our rucksacks, could you? I asked. So, with beaming faces of relief, we threw £1,000 worth of gear into the car of a complete stranger and waved him farewell. It would have made an interesting police report: "So, Mr Beard, how did he steal the articles?"
"Well, we opened the door and put them in his car."
We skipped merrily down the harsh gradients of the 2 miles to Suzie and Sandy in Stow (pronounced Stough as in Slough) where stranger and bags greeted us. We were knackered. The ankles were shot. We are not getting any better at this. Then the belt of rain swept in. The raindrops never reached the speed of Susie's ramblings as we ate the dinner she had made for us: we could nay fathom the accent, so we nodded and said "Really?" a lot when she infrequently paused for breath. We left for our early bed without a clue what she had said. Then we clicked: she had been a hairdresser!

## Day 49 Fri 6 May From Stow to North Middleton 13 miles

Happy 25th birthday James, it was great to chat to you and Bailey-the-planet-physicist (aged 4). We left our rucksacks at the B&B, walked the hilly lanes to North Middleton then caught the bus back to the B&B. It was the most strategic way of dealing with the remote route to Edinburgh, where we will make by tomorrow night after restarting at North Middleton. The threat of drizzle never did anything but it did not deter Cathy from being prepared. The waterproofs only served as something we could sweat in. My new boots behaved themselves, as did the cattle we helped to guide down the road with a young farmer or two. Plenty of young calves up there, so Cathy was particularly careful when crossing the fields once we left the lanes. When she saw the flimsy wiring (one weedy strand) at a large gap in the wall, Cathy broke into her Julia Bradbury strident paces because the bullocks still had their sweetmeats and looked menacing. It was rather late on in the walk when the defining moment of the day occurred. We saw Arthur's Seat below us. The asymmetric volcanic plug stood over its city with a regal air. A distinctive shape for the distinguished Edinburgh. We toddled to the A7 checked its pavements northwards then jumped on the 93 for an early rest. We even found a spare Daily Telegraph on the bus. Me and Cathy? Never a crossword.

## Day 50 Sat 7 May from North Middleton to Currie, Edinburgh 16 miles

Suzie had started the day with another lovely incomprehensible monologue covering several episodes in her life (we think) involving several people we had never heard of (we think). Cathy waited 20 minutes before there was enough of a break to ask for a piece of selotape. What great hospitality though. Sandy Aitcheson kindly found us a target B&B: The Riccarton Arms at Currie then offered to deliver our rucksacks. Today proved how high we were on the boarders. We walked 16 miles into Midlothian and it was all downhill. The gem of the area was Edinburgh whose castle we saw as we dropped from Gorebridge to Bonnyrigg. Until the last 2 miles it was a pavement walk alongside the main road from North Middleton's bus stop. So, with a fearful forecast proving once again toothless we carried waterproofs prudently (or needlessly) as we sped along impressively tree lined major routes. From the final 2 miles of our walk we found the Water Of Leith, a pushy peaty number from the Pentland Hills which we had walked around on today's toddle. The first spots of a long night of rain descended as we signed in at Currie. Inside were the riders of the parish boundary. The Burgh Of Biggar is probably the area or maybe the figurehead of the group. They had taken to horseback, around 20 of them of all ages to gallop their ground ("ride their marches") in keeping with a tradition I had never heard of. Cathy had. Once completed they all laughed a lot aided by vast quantities of alcohol.

## Day 51 Sun 8 May From Currie, Edinburgh to Nowhere, beyond Philpstoun   14 miles

If a man is short, fat and pushy there is never any need to add the word ignorant. Today's example found us at the breakfast table and proved he loved to talk about adders without the faintest idea how authoritatively stupid he sounded. We giggled for miles over "there are no adders now in Scotland" and "inbreeding killed them off" and "they wouldn't cross roads " and my personal favourite, " they wrap themselves around fishing rod handles" and the dumb defying "adders are most dangerous protecting their new borns in September!" Needless to say he gave us directions for our outward journey through Currie. We went the opposite way. So we found our way easily to the Union Canal once the rain had passed. We skipped a bend in the waterway by going into Broxburn just after the huge aqueduct over the River Almond and beyond the M8. The town's social club gave us free sandwiches as we told our tales to the locals. The slag heaps out of town had become the playground for scramble bike enthusiasts until the police turned up just before we did. The area looked great for the thrills but PC Plod was not seeing it that way. Rejoining the Canal at Whinchburg in the sunshine lightened my newly blistered feet (maybe these new boots were too cheap). We strode on further than we envisaged even after the late start. A lady from Boxted Essex walked with her son who recommended a chat with the farmer outside Philpstoun where caravans were stored. Success! A very kind lady permitted Cathy's high rucksack to smash bits off a barn door yet still allowed us to camp on thick, lush grass. As I hadn't brought my fishing rod we didn't need to fear adders!

## Day 52 Mon 9 May From Nowhere, beyond Philpstoun to Falkirk     14 miles

Our alarm clock was a donkey (or a Tony Adams look-a-like) making an ass of himself. The early morning saunter considered Cathy's feet (rather than mine for once), so we walked the lanes until Park Farm

Bridge. Here we rejoined The Union Canal (known as The Mathematical River for following the 240 ft. contour) that took us into delightful Linlithgow. Its Palace overlooking Loch Linlithgow was the birthplace of Scotland's James V and Mary Queen Of Scots. We refound the canal just over The River Avon (our third of that name) and never left it. Intermittent sun gave way to two bouts of drizzle without me needing to call on the cagoule and where the wind did blow, it did so in our favour. Therefore it was a good day for a walk on flat ground. The yellowhammer called for his first bit-of-bread-and-no-cheese as the heavy scent of may blossom overpowered the blue (and white) bells. The surprises at Falkirk were a 650 metre tunnel, a harlequin duck and the Falkirk Wheel. How many times have I stayed awake wandering how I would get my barge up 100ft. while bringing another down the opposite way? Well, no more sleepless nights for me. Modern engineering and old canals are an unlikely couple but they have a very civil partnership at The Falkirk Wheel where cradles of water (with or without boat) turn on a circle like a waterwheel. What was also impressive was the ease with which we got permission to camp in the grounds (fee waived) and given a key to the shower and toilet facilities. Thank you, Pauline. Black cloud showers hit us as soon as we had pitched. If the tent fails, we will sleep in the loos.

## Day 53 Tue 10 May From Falkirk to Kilsyth    10 miles

As we settled down last night a waterways' man wished us well as he left for home with the passing comment, "I'm sure you won't see bother tonight." Until then we felt safe. From then on there was always a fear that a nearby estate may spawn a knife-wielding gang of arsonists ready to fry a pre-wrapped couple. In truth we slept like logs and the overnight rain would have made the tent difficult to ignite. So the tent went in my rucksack infinitely heavier as a soggy lump. Cathy asked a man in the Wheel compound if there was a cafe in the next town to the west, Bonnie Bridge, and got a positive answer. We used the loos before dropping the key off at the security office where Cathy, ever vigilant that local advice we receive cannot always be trusted asked the security man if there was a cafe in Bonnie Bridge. What she did not recognise: it was the same man. Thankfully, humour emerged. The cafe was fine. We sat for 1 ½ hours as more rain passed through, then returned to the new canal: The Forth (Bonnie) and Clyde Canal. It was a bigger version of The Union built for sea-going vessels to reach Falkirk. It was soon mundane though. The smaller canal had developed a corridor of nature whereas this one had found more constant use it would seem. Mind you, the fishing was better. Cathy told the angler he had a bite as he talked to us. A perch of nearly one pound proved the point as more rain swept in. The wet stuff kept doing that. We had enough of the weather and my side strain showed signs of spasm so I got the sympathy vote after 10 miles at Kilsyth. (Cathy had been telling me of it for some time but I had been ignoring her.) Sadly, the Coachman Hotel was 1 ½ km. uphill off our route which we will need to retrace tomorrow but it gave us a rest from pushing into that westerly wind. Once in the privacy of our room (I must add) I stripped to reveal a lop-sidedness, caused by the 'side strain' that made the Leaning Tower of Pisa look upright. Cathy got concerned that the instability at the bottom of my body (my ankles) and at the top of me (my instable brain) had now got a mid range partner with my unstable hip. There must have been a fear that all the bits of instability would join up and I would end up as a pool of shivering ectoplasm. At this point she called our osteopath, Jim McAvoy; he inspired her to try manipulating my sacrum. Oh er!? So there we were, on the hotel bed performing acts that were somewhat outside my preferred options. No luck so Plan B: a 10am appointment with Robert Clarke, osteopath, somewhere near a Chinese Takeaway in Cumbernauld.

## Day 54 Wed 11 May From Kilsyth to Kirkinillock  5 miles

Early breakfast, then the number 43 bus to Cumbernauld's shopping centre which did not appear on our original route but did highlight most of the deficiencies of early 1970's architecture. Robert Clarke's acts were less delicate than Cathy's and as a consequence, my back felt far too pulverised to know whether the treatment had been worthwhile. "24 to 48 hours complete rest, then 5 to 10 days to get full recovery," Robert told me. So, after an afternoon nap, we walked 5 miles along the canal to Kirkintilloch. I can't say I galloped but the theory was that walking straightens my body out so I gave it a go. Apart for the rain it went well. The hawthorn blossom stayed unopened, that is how dull the weather was. The only colour was the cow-parsley lining the hedgerows and the only person we saw other than commuter cyclists was a gun dog trainer with two handsome pointers. Cathy kept checking I was being sensible with my back and I was attempting to convince her I was. By making it to Kirkintilloch we had sliced an original day's walk into two leaving a slightly longer half for tomorrow. We could afford the delay whilst building up my back's strength. I had done enough for the day to feel some success. Time for a Thai curry! One of the reasons for not eating again in our hotel was the music. Not that jazz/ funk doesn't have its place, it just should not be played so loud. After one Guinness last night, I said to the barman, "We may have had another but for the music". Yet, once more at breakfast (yes, breakfast) we had to asked for it to be turned down when we were the only ones in the restaurant. We were hardly going to strut our stuff over poached eggs, so why boom the disco beat? Hey, we <u>are</u> getting old!

## Day 55 Th 12 May From Kirkinillock to Strathblane 8 miles

Cathy spent all last night ringing all the B&Bs or campsites on our West Highland Way trek as well as A.M.S, our bag carriers. Our path is laid out for the next 9 days. So plod No1 was 8 miles from yesterday's punctuation mark to Strathblane. It had not been a good night's sleep due to hot flushes and manipulation aches, so we were tense. Cathy told it like she saw it then love reigned again. The fine path was an old railway line blessed with many streams, trees and rural vistas under The Campsie Fells. The weather was less blessed but the trees protected us from the brunt of it and we managed it in 2 ½ steady hours without undue stress on my back (we hope). The final two miles took us around a rocky scar that signalled the terrain we are likely to face ahead. The Kirkhouse Hotel shocked us. Over the phone the room rate was £50 but this luxury building, established in 1601, was finely decked out as we toddled in like vagabonds into a palace and noticed single room prices starting at £75, doubles at £125. "Excuse us, how much are we paying?" We had to ask. "£50. Food is available until...." Well, well. The Cross Keys in rotten Walsden can stick his £55 cardboard-box-room right where it hurts. This was cheap luxury. Tasteful sofa and soft furniture, a large dressing table under the five windowed bay overlooking the hills, one monster bed and a sumptuous corner bath in the en-suite. Yes, I think we will take it.

There was another game to be played, though. Our waterproof trousers are not. No. Not very. So we tracked down some Paramo proper ones in Stirling. Yes, the town we have travelled a further 13 miles from only today. Cathy allowed me to rest as she spent 3 ½ hours on buses and at bus stations on this expedition. Success! Great trews. Cathy deserved pampering and the inn's steak night was just the ticket.

## Day 56 Fri 13 May From Strathblane to Croftburn 5 miles

Not a good day. It started well enough. Breakfast of kipper and smoked salmon with the old scramblies. Back to bed until the eleven o'clock check out. However, after a last minute bath, I stepped on the rubber bath mat and thumped down the step in the bathroom. I only jarred the right leg. I didn't even fall down, but the sciatic nerve took a twang. We got a few miles down The West Highland Way (sweet though it was) when Cathy convinced me to give up at least for the day. How do we get to the osteopath in Cumbernauld? Bus to Glasgow, then out? Where do we get the bus? From The Glen Goyne Distillery. Missed it. Cathy saw a couple leaving the distillery so asked if they were going our way. No, they were the owners (Stuart and wife) who called for a taxi on their account. Even with pain ripping down my leg, I put on a smile. I was so annoyed with myself. Cathy concurred. Robert Clarke cranked my back again. With more sympathy than I deserved. My back was weaker than ever, so the synopsis is /was not great. The taxi driver waited for us and we paid cash for the return trip beyond the distillery to our prearranged B&B near Drymen. We needed to hole up for a day or two and unpick all The West Highland Way route we (or rather Cathy) worked so hard to organise yesterday. Not a good day.

## Day 57 Sat 14 May From Croftburn to Strathblane
### 0 inches (torn back muscle)

I am so annoyed with myself for that careless slip. Always will be. The only good thing that happened to us today was our departure from our B&B. The libel laws will not allow me to name John and Eileen Reid as the crabbiest B&B people in the world. There are so many issues I can only give the final insult. The out-of-the-way nature of the place meant their "pick-up and drop-off" was "all part of the deal," John said. As we were not asking to be dropped off in the same place as the pick-up, we offered to take a bus. "No problem," said John, "I can take you, " ...dither.. "or Ellen..." dither.. "or me..." change of mind ... dither. Then, just as we were leaving, he asked for £5 petrol money. Bearing in mind, his dreary B&B was £10 per night more than the fine hotel room of The Kirkhouse Inn we were running back to, this was some cheek! I did not mention the free taxi from the distillery, yesterday. Good old Cathy, she only had £4.93 in her pocket, yet she insisted she went in search of the other 7p, just to rub their noses in their pettiness. They could never be embarrassed, though, over something as important as 7p!! Anyhow, they never got it but we got back to The Kirkhouse Inn who did everything they could to put me into a bed as soon as the cleaners could make it possible. My pain was bad and Cathy suffered my moaning for two days (I am into the third as I write, but the agony has now turned to an ache). Rumours that I was skiving only to watch the FA Cup Final were scotched by local TV overriding English TV up here. Dichlofenac and cocodamol tablets were being fired in as regularly as my nurse Cathy would allow. Osteo Robert had said the second day would be the worst and I don't know how that worked but he was right.

## Day 58 Sun15 May  Stayed in Strathblane 0 inches
## (torn back muscle)

My Dad would have been 89 today. He died over 30 years ago, not many days older than I am today. He was a great man and a constant inspiration to me. So, as a wimp with a bad back today, I felt a failure. That's when Cathy was needed most. I was grinding teeth, grabbing at my thigh where the nerve gave me stabbing pains and generally I was not a happy bunny. It was lovely to get a call from Laura because I needed to give her an upbeat scenario about my recovery as she worries about her Dad. Lord knows I have given plenty of reasons for that in the past. Laura and bump were well. That picked me up. I stayed awake with Match of The Day on to watch Spurs beat Liverpool 2-0 but Scottish TV was only covering Ranger's league title, so that got me stoked up. An awful early-hour night turned better by the morning. At first I thought it was only the painkillers.

## Day 59 Mon 16 May  Stayed in Strathblane 0 inches
## (torn back muscle)

I feel less pain! A chat with Osteo Robert over the phone made me realise I would need two more days of rest but, as my spine is straight, it would be likely that the soft tissue could heal enough to resume walking by Wednesday (or more treatment). Cathy was getting cabin crazy but still doing everything for me.

## Day 60 Tue 17 May From Strathblane to Drymen 5 miles

A little walk without my legs falling off! Just the 5 miles I failed to complete on Friday's walk, but it was a far cry from my despair over the weekend. The bus dropped us at Glen Goyne's Distillery for us to rejoin the West Highland Way (WHW) at The Beech Tree Inn. It followed an old railway track for a few miles in grey weather that topped out the mountains at 2,000ft. We got our first sight of Loch Lomond and a few of its southern islands before descending into Drymen. Cathy's back got a twinge. No worry, she's more resilient than this wimp. Vegetable curry and Belhave bitter proved a potent force. It was Glasgow strength that provided a night-long gassy blow-back worthy of a cow-shed. Cathy was an innocent bystander (for once) who, unfortunately suffered in the cross fire.

## Day 61 Wed 18 May From Drymen to Rowardennan YHA, Loch Loman 11 miles

Why are curries just as hot on the way out as they are on the way in? Back to the walking after a dash to the docs for a painkiller prescription and a donation from the chemist. Both backs stood up to the 11 mile trek along Loch Lomond from Drymen to Rowardennan on the eastern bank under the beady eye of Ben Lomond's 3,000ft.-plus massif when it was not carpeted in rain. Westerly squalls swept over us throughout the day, creating a constant attack of waves along the shore line. When the sun flourished, so did the dramatic colour-scheme. None more so than the bluebells that thrived in all the glorious woodland that held us for most of the way. The bullfinch ran them close. Not as common as yesteryear, he gave us a fine display as did a pair of red-breasted mergansers hunting in the shallows. A coffee-lunch at Balmaha was the only true rest we took so we must have walked well, even though it was disappointing to note our feet began to hurt. The bruises must have been deep. On the plus side (and there is so much) is the vastness of the scenery. This is now very grand indeed. Looks like we are back on track. To end the day, two goosanders swam by the hostel as lamb steaks sizzled. The night proved weird. We were split into boy/girl dorms and the final 5$^{th}$ and 6$^{th}$ guys to doss down in my dorm had been down the pub. They snored as a duet. It proved too much for me. I'd enough trouble with the trapped nerve down my right leg, so I wandered to Cathy's dorm, tapped timidly on the door until she stirred. Fortunately no one else had joined her, so I dragged my bedclothes along the corridor and sneaked in.

## Day 62 Thu 19 May From Rowardennan YHA, Loch Loman to Inveranan 14 miles

"Milestones" have been great on this walk, so it was a proud moment when we declared we had "walked the length of Loch Lomond." Bloody relieved, too. It was a shocking walk. We knew the two 7mile sections were known to be tough but some bright burk (me) suggested putting them together in one day. It rained off and on all day so, as all seasoned fell-walkers can testify, after a week of precipitation, all becks (burns) were covered with water. In fact, even the occasional flat path could have been declared a mountain stream. We forded many rivulets by make-shift stepping stones, swinging along fences, hop-skip and jumping or just plain wading. Yet the water was nothing compared to the rocky terrain. Each headland that protruded into the lake had crags of significant boulders (and sneaky smaller blighters) that littered the way. Tree roots were far from useful as well. So, for 8 of our 14 miles, we scrambled at around 1 mph; picking our way along the line of the loch at anything from the waterline or on towering traverses 200ft. above it. At first we considered this to be 'technical rambling', but after a while we just wanted it to end. The remote mid-way hotel (Inversaid Hotel) was naff (our lunch appeared in a bag) but the giggles helped us through the next hour's slog. Three miles beyond the loch, over a hill to the next glen, was the fabulous campsite of Beinglas in Inverannan. The bhuna curry was saturated in taste, predominately coriander and garlic, and only 13 yards from our tent. The Macallum malt night-capped a challenging day. Boy, we did sleep well. Rain, what rain?

We walked the complete length of Loch Lomond. Mainly underwater.

### Day 63 Fri 20 May   From Inveranan to Tyndrum 12 miles

The rain had swollen the River Falloch to its gushing gunnels. The same went for every burn in the glen, so we walked upstream, north westwards so the stream skills learnt yesterday were back in action. The tracks, however were better underfoot as we followed the contours of the hills along the valley. The overnight rain had fallen as snow on the higher mountains: Ben More and Stob Bullein among them. These created fine backdrop scenery to the wide expanse of the splendour of the Glen. Chats with other walkers had become common place and the same faces were seen and reseen. The Dutch and Germans are plentiful but Austrians and Australians are here too

. So are two chaps who we have observed for three hours on three separate occasions. They have not said one word to each other! Maybe David at Tyndrum's Paddy Bar had taken their share of words. His demonstration to Cathy of how to drink malt whisky became very fluid. Too much Springbank, excellent though it was, gave Cathy a bad headache overnight. Furthermore it poured throughout. Rain, not whisky.

*Was Robert The Bruce the first man to be inspired by a web-site?*

## Day 64 Sat 21 May   From Tyndrum to Inveroran 11 miles

A wet tent got packed then we got an early coffee and roll in Tyndrum before we set off under clouds that decapitated the mountains at 1,500 ft. While light veils of dissipating cloud lifted from the highland woodlands, the distant views were never clear all day. Gentle rain came off and on all morning and a storm force wind brought the heavy artillery that never stopped from lunchtime. Fortunately it was a straight forward trek with only one fellside that was scree strewn. The rest was stone tracked on reasonable gradients. For this reason, I guess, it attracted the walking families out from Glasgow that leapt off the train at Tyndrum and skipped through the waterlogged glens to Orchy where the hotel was a fab place to stop. The wind whipped us in and nearly kept us in, but they were full. The portents of doom lay in every weather forecast so wild camping begun to dwindle as a romantic option. The landlady was very helpful and phoned a friend, Maurice, who would take us in at his cottage at the top of Tullach Loch, just where we needed to be. The three miles up the river and through Caledonian pine along the length of the loch would have been idyllic. In torrential rain it was pants. Maurice was our age, lived alone with Buzz his border collie and all his fishing rods (Maurice's not Buzz's) on the living room walls. The main ingredient in the hotel's chowder that night was Maurice's salmon caught from the Tay nearby. If we had insisted on venison I dare say he would have impinged upon one of several red deer that passed within seven yards of his arm chair. Torrential rain thrashed his cottage to within an inch of its life but it was used to that. The campers by the river were less fortunate but benefited from the estate's gamekeeper who sent them to higher ground before the raging torrent rose. If those banks collapsed there would be no government bail out! Our bedroom view took in the fell opposite with various levels of horizontal precipitation in the evening lights, 'the gloaming', that held to beyond 10-30.

## Day 65 Sun 22 May From Inveroran to King's House Hotel, in the glen    10 miles

An amber weather forecast had been issued for the next two days (extended to three and counting later). We set off by 9-00 to catch what lesser weather we could. In the past I have driven three times over or round Rannoch Moor and always felt it was the bleakest place in the kingdom. As we ascended through scattered showers with occasional sunshine I was delighted by the isolation and the vastness of its wilderness: way, way beyond the A82. Big mountains towered in every direction over ling heather marginalised by countless tarns / lochans of every contorted shape. Then came the 50mph winds. Then the rain that crackled on the anorak hood like an old radio out of tune. Any direct-hit on the skin stung. I then realised that my first impressions of Rannock Moor had been confirmed. A rapid descent to King's House Hotel followed, nothing could keep Cathy warm, so her temperature plummeted in the weather. The remote hotel (complete with its own herd of red deer- or 'lunch') could not have been more needed. It was early afternoon when we got into bed. Sleet fell (was thrown) and the Air Force Mountain Rescue helicopter landed outside. The amber weather warning had been proved right.

## Day 66 Mon 23 May From King's House Hotel to Kinlochleven 9 miles

For me, this was the most exhilarating day's walk of the whole campaign. However, as the most stupid, dangerous and risky exercise, there were moments when Cathy withheld her full concurrence. Going over Glencoe's Devil's Staircase, a mountain pass at around 2,000 ft, when sea level winds reached 70mph, meant walkers were thrown over. The Barrow Boys said two were blown over, one like "a rag doll". That may have been Brian who had his legs thrown over his head and sent tumbling yards down heather thankfully when all around was rocky. I got pushed over but we felt we got away without damage by being 40 minutes ahead of the worst on top. Even so, we needed to bend into the tripod position using a walking pole as a prop or hung onto each other as a double tripod!! We were pushed around from the off and soon gave up trying to cross streams dry footed. Dozens of becks had been created from the bad weather that even locals felt was the most severe for years. We powered to the base of the pass with a break in the rain misguiding us into optimism with just the wind to deal with. The vast glens told us more driving rain was heading our way, hitting us just before the top. Cathy's swearing kept her going and convinced me she was never going to be beaten. Just battered. Kinlochleven, our destination was at sea level so it was a lengthy descent. The south-westerlies swirled rather than blasted by the time we had dropped to 1,000ft so we afforded a reassuring kiss. Just as we got to our hostel the big winds wound up even bigger! We had just made a cuppa when the electricity went. No one was surprised. The hydro-electric pipes are just outside, can't we just plug in? The whole area for 40 miles around was out of electricity for 8 hours, other areas for over a day. Dinner was courtesy of the gas cooker in the McDonald's hotel. There were tales of ripped jackets, tents with their contents blown away and tents in trees. Winds of 110mph were recorded.

## Day 67 Tue 24 May From Kinlochleven to Fort William 14 miles

This would have been horrendous weather if yesterday had not happened. The hailstorms were like gunshot. But our hoods had been set to downward looking slots. The route was steep but we were ready for a fight. Good fun, really, in stunning highland scenery although it did go grey, even black and watery for long periods. 1,000ft shoots of water cascaded as continuous waterfalls from all the peaks. Streams were everywhere and our feet were soon soaked. Several pines had been felled by yesterday's storm: 40ft blighters. We knew we had witnessed something mighty. Through the showers, we got to Fort William with even a glimpse of both sun and Ben Nevis. We completed The West Highland Way (I think they lost the S while we walked it) and felt duly proud. New innov8 shoes were bought in celebration and a touch of necessity. The forecast put us into a B&B. The rest of the night was spent on the phone to Great Glen Way B&B's; all of whom were fully booked. Back to the walk and Cathy's gloves: I had questioned bringing them. Well, without them, Cathy would not have made it over the WHW passes. Long Live The Gloves.

## Day 68 Wed 25 May From Fort William to Gairlochy 10 miles

It rained for most of the walk but, given the last four days, we did not notice. We began The Great Glen Way with Ben Nevis lifting her skirt sufficiently to expose her petticoat of snow, yet we never got to her garter-line. No sun at all, only a modicum of breeze and a path to match. No surprise after recent terror-trekking. Things looked up when we did. The distant views included some of the harshest mountainsides imaginable but the sequence of Telford locks called Neptune Staircase only impressed on an engineering basis. It would be harsh to say it for many reasons, but they were hardly a National Wonder. The four cruising boats we saw over our 9 mile walk were not manned by anyone enjoying themselves. Mind you. The Germans walking on from the WHW are hardly in the Premier Chuckle League. Still, it did give Cathy and me something to (privately) insult. It was that kind of day.

## Day 69 Thu 26 May From Gairlochy to Laggan 13 miles

What is it with Germans cleaning their teeth for 15 minutes?
Sad for us, the midges have arrived. Slightly happier for Cathy, they prefer biting me to her.
Once we got going we realised midges don't bother with moving targets. This was one of the reasons we hardly stopped all day. Another was the fear that the Chattering Classes might catch up with us. From inside our tent last night we heard the drone of their dreary voices skimming over grey subjects without pause or hesitation, so we ran scared. Another was (I can hardly bring myself to write this again) that it rained almost all day. So, no sun lounging. The walk itself was from the Caledonian Canal's western end to Laggan Locks. In between was Loch Lochy which consumed our day as we walked its northern bank. This was a modern bank, like the Nat West Tower: high-rise, so we were often 100ft above the water. To continue the analogy: we could not see the wood for the trees (is that sub-prime debt looking good in the Scotch mist?). The forestry commission put paid to most of the views and drizzle virtually smothered the rest. Just occasionally, the glimpse of the loch-life lifted us, with suspended white clouds against high, long ridges. Yet too rarely. Cathy reckoned it was the dreariest day's walk to date. That was harsh, but the factors mounted in her favour. At least we walked fast enough to avoid the ring-tones and talk of the price of pink wellies. Cathy was knackered. Recent days had taken their toll. Lots of food and sleep were needed. A pasta-bake plus haggis and beans were heaped as a main course with a bar of whole nut chocolate each to

follow. She was asleep by 5pm. I woke her at 7 but the zeds found her again by 9 and held her hostage until 7a.m.

## Day 70 Fri 27 May From Laggan to Augustus   10 miles

Dehydration probably caused Cathy's headache but love and breakfast got her chirpy as a chipmunk by the time we strode out. Rain avoided us today but the sun never broke the cloud's headlock. Our own loch ahead was Loch Oich (true) which fell east from the watershed at Laggan. The incised valley widened and each ridge had reduced but the disused Mulgarry and Augustus railway line provided enough deciduous scenery to be one up on yesterday. Our 10$^{th}$ cuckoo (yep, counting cuckoos-do you reckon we have cracked!) was around for the morning and we were obviously too close to an oystercatcher's nest at one point. Boy, they yell. Unlike the dipper that stood on a Canute-throne rock, cool as could be as we passed within 6ft. Fort Augustus appeared and so did a road, therefore tourists were everywhere within 200 yards of a car park. None had been seen on the footpath. This was the western end of Loch Ness and the monsters were plentiful, mainly buying local shortbread biscuits or an imitation sporran for the wall above the Frank Sinatra LP's. We brought the best steak in the butchers and hid from the oncoming rain at the fine hostel. Mr. Harlow said his tent was getting soggy. He had our sympathy. We had our own room indoors.

## Day 71 Sat 28 May From Fort Augustus to Alltsigh 10 miles

This was my first true sight of Loch Ness and it was monstrous. The walk was high above the water within the pines and larches of the Forestry Commission that only parted where felling had recently taken place. This gave us a few good views of the wide expanse of wind-whipped loch under the uninhabited slopes of the southern shore, but there were too many trees to see the sights we knew were out there. The showers were heavier but they were traded in for bright sunshine every 20 minutes. We side-tracked down to Invermoriston only to find several 50feet-high pines had become 50 feet –*long* pines. Their uprooting forced us to scrabble over moss-walls, under deer fencing and through rain soaked bushes. I was petulantly starving, so the Invermoriston got our custom before we stroked reindeer hides in the craft shop. More tree-blind hillsides got us to Alltsigh where a B&B got preference over a Scottish Youth Hostel that did not understand walkers (or the British). It was also closed until 5-00 and we certainly didn't fancy waiting in the pouring rain for 2 hours. We pined for a dry bed.

## Day 72 Sun 29 May From Alltsigh to Milton, outside Drumnadrochit 12 miles

Duncan McKenzie donned his family-tartan kilt and full accessories including a 4 foot sword "for Nessie fighting", then served our breakfast overlooking the famous loch. The Great Glen Way took us higher than ever, well, for this glen. At 1,000ft., the trees were eventually cleared to give us a view over the first ridge to several ranges, one after another. Sadly, the haze of drizzle that arrived in waves from the west never allowed a full panoramic view in total clarity but we got a sense of grandeur of a mighty place. This tectonic fault is still moving apart at 1 cm. per year so we have not seen it at its widest but it is a monster. Bright broom had gorse to compete for brightest yellow on the block and the pines were tinged with their new green hair- extensions. So sun at last, if only for moments, as we turned away from the Great Glen at the wonderfully named Drumnadrochit. The steep descent into the town and into a divine B&B in nearby Milton meant that the next day's start would be severely uphill out of the green valley. A harsh wind and lashing rain drove us to our welcome refuge. Perhaps I can mention our silly singing that occurs most days. It starts later in the day, as it did so today. We were still high up but round the blind side of the hill, so the loch was unseen.

We passed two lochan, and then it was a lane plod as we recalled "How Much Was That Doggy In The Window?" Schoolboy humour took over when we failed to recall the verses and we giggled as we came up with:

> I don't want a shag or a cormorant
> I can't get the horn of a bull
> A pussy could even turn smelly
> A cock would be no good at all!

## Day 73 Mon 30 May From Milton, outside Drumnadrochit to Muir of Ord 15 miles

"Not more f'ing rain," yelled Cathy as a familiar cascade hit us just as we had left the B&B after early morning sun. This was the heaviest and most prolonged of four showers on a day which was bathed in sunshine for the remainder. It just happened when we were reacquainting ourselves with our full-payload-rucksacks as well as tackling the steep Glen Conwinth Road rising 800ft. Despite the early dilution it was a good walk over high moorland swathed in winter-wear heather and stands of deciduous trees in fresh leaf. For the past week the hooded crow has replaced the carrion fella. We had too charming close encounters with busy female blackcaps and our first sighting on this walk of a tree creeper that nearly joined us for dinner of Ceylon curry as we sat on a bench 4 feet from the Beauly salmon river. A further nugget in today's pan was the discovery of Abbot Ale on tap at The Kiltanlilty Hotel, our pit stop. The change in scenery uplifted us, but that may have been aided by the better weather. This encouraged us to camp without fear of ending up in the trees. We pitched at Lovat Bridge, near Beauly, a pretty town named by Mary Queen of Scots. We left our kit at the tent and walked for a further 4 miles, then got the bus back. That will save us a dreary road walk tomorrow. It also got us a curry take away, as aforementioned, eaten in evening sunshine. Red sky at night is encouraging. I hope it will mean Cathy won't be swearing tomorrow.

## Day 74 Tue 31 May  From Muir of Ord to Alness 17 miles

The Northern tilt is working now so we have midnight sun. Sadly, though, it was broad daylight at 4am when the crows round here had a squabble. I wanted to murder them, collectively. Local knowledge failed as usual: no bus, so a taxi got us to our restart and three miles on we found a coffee shop in Conan Bridge instead of none as previously informed. It was after cappuccinos and between fish tanks that we changed from waterproofs into shorts. In lighter attire and bright daylight we strode the lanes to Dingwall to discover the world's least efficient post office. Cathy's reaction, after queuing for an inordinate length of time, to a post office without envelopes for sale was to establish just how miserable the assistant could be. Cathy attempted to buy a lone, unattached envelope from the sparsely occupied card-stand. The refusal led to a piece of Cathy's mind being given with a few 'hear-hear's' from the locals. It took a few days for the smoke to clear. Fiery, when stirred, my gal. We lifted to a height of 300ft. above the elongated estuary containing a portable oil-rig in storage. The gentler hills of the rich coastal farmland could have been Suffolk if you failed to spin west to see a patch of snow on the fells. It would have been extremely pleasant but for the cars, three in particular. Two were driven too fast by young men (in flashy cars) with just enough intelligence to think they were as stupid as Jeremy Clarkson. The other was a druggie or drunk or both who hit the grass verge just before us and bounced across the road past us. Sunshine at Evanton convinced us to pitch a tent, and then walk onto Alness along the cycle track beside the B817 without our packs. This efficient use of the evening light and local buses felt quite good at the time but the latter stroll meant less recovery time. It also meant a pub dinner in the Novar Arms Hotel and a dram of the malt (Dalmore) that brought on Cathy's headache overnight. Cathy deserved the whisky, not the headache.

## Day 75 Wed 1 June From Alness to Tain 13.5 miles

Overnight rain was followed by dark clouds threatening from the west yet they never delivered more than spots of rain and pre-emptive wind. It took a late breakfast and a strong pill to tackle Cathy's piecing headache by which time we had forwarded our bags to our Tain B&B and resumed our walk where we had left off last night on Alness High Street. The first of the month brought the first eider ducks and the first foxgloves. There was more broom sweeping across the countryside than I had ever seen before but it was not the only yellow to paint the slopes. Rape seed was still in bloom in large fields similar to back home. The whole walk was rural; there were no settlements between Alness and Tain on the hillside-lane alternative to the A9. So no coffee shops. I'd never been a big fan until this adventure and now I see them as havens; a chance for a rest. The previous two evening walks were taking their toll even without carrying rucksacks so we cheered ourselves up by rolling our waterproofs above our knees, wore knotted handkerchiefs on our heads, clenched our fists and walked on saying "Der" a lot. "Gumbos", Cathy called us. As soon as a car came we felt guilty enough to hide our hankies and look normal (ish). Local info. and O.S. maps continued to be absent even in The Royal Burgh of Tain, home of the Glenmorangie Distillery.

Then there was the oddity of the Dunbuis B&B: an automatic light in the en-suite facilities: it worked on one's initial and subsequent movement (excluding bowel). However once the shower cubicle misted up, the sensor could not register my existence so I was suddenly in the dark and I had to call Cathy to come in to turn it back on. The light of my life.

*Tain Centre: Is that where the Queen goes shopping?*

## Day 76 Thu 2 June From Tain to the shoreline of Loch Fleet 12.5 miles

Our first day without rain since May 5th. We left Tain by its northern route, wondering if the local guy named Edward was tainted. This was our first stretch on a major road, the A9. It had a wide verge of tarmac, ordinarily for cyclists, and the traffic was not onerous but the speed of the steel was fast enough to scare us when it's that close. We always stopped still for lorries as their air wakes were considerable, especially in the gusty south-westerly of the day. Crossing the 2km of the Donar Bridge over the raging tide of The Dornoch Firth caused a further stir due to Cathy's fear of heights. We strode strongly as I held the sweetest palm ever. Once over, we left the A9 for a gorse-lined heathland track eastwards along the bay. We found where all the yellowhammers had disappeared to. An invite for a coffee or beer came to us from touring caravanners Brian and Bridget then we pressed onto Dornoch (I know, we should have pressed onto Doorbell). Light lunch and another entertaining bout of Cathy hating humans. This time she was delayed by a fat family choosing 2 pies and three cakes each! A country lane got us over the land for the descent to the next Loch (Fleet). This natural wonder got in our way. A 50 yard non-crossing meant an 8 mile round trek. It was on these shores we wild camped, hoping it wasn't to be a spring tide. The day's wildlife included a brown argos (not the shop), a seal (not the singer), eider ducks (who weren't down) and flocks of waders (not being worn by anglers). The grunts close to our tent were deemed to be otters (not our snoring).
I will not tell jokes about steps of wood over a fence.
It's just not my stile.

## Day 77 Fri 03 June From the shoreline of Loch Fleet to Dalchaim near Bora 13 miles

It was a game of two halves. We left our flattened grass patch and soon engaged the torrid A9 where the side of the road was the edge of the road. If you get the dangerous picture. Cathy's language quickly became industrial, particularly at anybody overtaking behind or alongside us. Appeasement could only be made over a breakfast that lasted 1 ½ hours involving newspapers and good coffee in quantity. Whilst reading, Cathy's glasses broke but fortune smiled as an Aladdin's cave sold the only specs for miles around. Cathy, without glasses to read the maps would be as devastated as I would be without my pen! The sun burnt brightly all day, so the second half's grassy coastal path from Gospie was a dream.

Cathy coasting

The North Sea was not only calm but crystal clear. Grey seals followed us from bay to bay and ringed plovers warned us away from their nests just above the high-water line. Fabulous fulmars did the same around their nests on sandstone cliffs, just more acrobatically. One crofter was crabby; the older one was delighted to see us despite reminding him of widowhood. We had passed the Earl Of Sutherland's Dunrobin Castle in all its splendour just after Golspie but the natural beauty of the rarely trodden coast was the day's winner. Beyond Brora (a town gradually closing down), we found a tiny coastal campsite, unattended with the only sign of life being a radio turned to the Test Match. Our kinda folks.

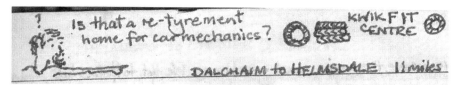

## Day 78 Sat 4 June from Dalchaim near Bora to Helmsdale 11 miles

3-45am: we were awake. 4-15 are. We were walking the A9. So that's how it was. Cloud cover, a cool north-easterly (after a blast last night) and a sun up there somewhere. At least it was traffic-free. We strode out before the boy- racers saw their coco-pops, so it was a safe walk by comparison to any previous A9 experience. We were getting the job done in our own, determined fashion. The cuckoos helped, so did the powder-grey sea with its barking seal pups; but achieving the mileage was what mattered. We would get better conditions for countryside walking once we wave the main road goodbye. We got to Helmsdale, found a hotel that served breakfast for non-residents and were told that breakfast started at 8am. We'd arrived before 7-30! Next job was setting up for tomorrow by taking our bags 15 miles on so we could walk light. Before we got the bus to Dunbeath, a couple we had met 4 days ago in the Novar Arms in Alness, offered us a lift there. All we had to do was listen to local history tales. We were grateful for their kindness as it gave us time to find the campsite, leave our rucksacks and have soup from a man who owned Oregan Trail, the 1981 Arkle winner at Cheltenham. Back to Helmsdale, we climbed out of the town up a hill overlooking an expanse of sea that must see its fair share of whales. It certainly had enough gannets. All this from the window of Burnside B&B. We did not need a telly...........especially as England v Switzerland soccer was not shown on Scottish ITV.

## Day 79 Sun 5 June   From Helmsdale to Lybster   23 miles

On our way by 4-30am. Eight red deer were grazing on the lane's verge and only begrudgingly trotted off into the heathered hills. We saw two further herds close by the A9, all of whom looked at us like we should not be there at that time in the morning. I would have normally agreed but I felt very alive in the freshness of a new dawn. Cathy, of course was her usual strident self as we took the line of the old A9 until it rejoined the new section high on the next promontory north of Helmsdale. We found a good pace without our full payloads, so we soon swept past the cotton-grass covered moors then down and up the Berriedale Braes. These infamous, steep hills came easy to us under the more persistent sun; therefore we looked fresh when we stopped to chat with 3 cyclists on their morning No. 1 of 10 going the other way. I mistook the elegant, slender black guy in black lycra for a stick of liquorice. It takes all sorts. Suddenly, there was Dunbeath: 15 miles in 5 hours with stops included. Most importantly, it was achieved safely due to the early start. Bacon rolls and coffee at the campsite were provided in the owner's house with the lady ready to go to church. A two hour rest perked us up for Sunday lunch at Trevor's including local lobster and three pints of Trade Wind bitter. I don't know who I was supposed to trade mine with. The verve of the moment got us to walk 8 miles to Lybster to aid the final push. A great black-backed gull mobbed a buzzard for our entertainment in the evening sun, and then we bussed back to Dunbeath's base camp.

### Day 80 Mon   06 June From Lybster to a croft 4 miles beyond Watten 18.5 miles

A murder of crows witnessed the murder of a crow as a herring gull seized a chick from nearby nests and flew by our tent to avoid the angry mob that yelled and wheeled in pursuit. Our own breakfast came much easier: in the site-owner's house again. The bus halted at our arm with no need for a bus-stop, so we were in Lybster for a 9-50 start. Yesterday's mileage (23 miles) could be felt in our legs as we cleared the last of the A roads we were likely to see on the east coast and took the refreshingly peaceful lane north to Watten, passing the Camster burial cairns on the way. The bodies were left in a sitting position in the round chambers. It was not mentioned whether they were part of a séance, trying to get in touch with themselves. We were in lowlands. I am sure Cathy said the geographical term was flow, but the last few days on the A9 had generated plenty of "f"s. The classically shaped mountains could be seen in the far west of our panorama, one of which was Morven. 14 miles in we took milky coffee at The Brown Trout Hotel on Loch Watten (no bar open until 5-00). This would have been enough on most days but this was our next-to-last day and we wanted tomorrow's walk to be relatively easy, so we pressed on for another 4. Within a mile of leaving the hotel a guy offered a cuppa. It turned out he had done the same to the naked rambler and his girlfriend when they were completing the LEJO one February. Everything was blue, he reckoned. We pressed on to camp on a kind crofter's lawn just 15 miles short of John O'Groats. It looks like another cold night but nothing will stop us now. Well, unless the Highland bull gets loose. We met the couple's son, a burly 30-something, who like many of his generation, had expressed his intelligence and sensitivity by stapling several lumps of metal to his face. His function in life was to ride his quad bike to every corner of the croft to hug each of "the pets we eat." He maintained this activity beyond 11pm. in this land of the midnight sun until he accidently let one out (animal, not fart). This created lots of shouting and limping down the lane. I forgot to say: his Dad lived on crutches as a result of a goring by the said beast. After these tales, Cathy was never going to let me help (thank Christ). From a quivering position inside our tent, there were fears that we could be trampled to death with just one day to go! The mother eventually chained her lad up, it seemed, to a post utilising one of the rings through his nose.

## Day 81 Tue 07 June From a croft 4 miles beyond Watten to John O'Groats 15 miles

John O'Groats: We made it! What an awful day to end with. Rain delayed the start until 9-20am and drizzle drifted across too many times thereafter as straight roads and flat moorland served up one of the dullest day's foot slog of the 81 we have taken. It was cold enough for Cathy to wear gloves. This was my last opportunity to talk to the fellow bent-noses, the curlews. I was trying to sing the la-la-la section of The Proclaimers' "I will walk 500 miles", but they took it to be a competition. With no self respecting swallow out on such a day, the kestrels ruled the air. Cold air. It blasted us from the east, so it was hard work, the famous line, "this might be the last hill we see today", got trotted out ten times. Then "At least it's not raining," brought on the rain. This was a slog. Rather fitting, really, as we would not want to forget that every day was tough. We fought for the mileage. So why wasn't it sunny for the big ending? We did not need one. It was the whole walk that was big. Our time together had been wonderful. The sights and people had been very special. So, when we got to the famous John O Groat's signpost and the money grabbing photographer said it was his post so we would have to pay him for a photo because we weren't allowed to take our own, we realised there were still some small minds about. Just three paces away were bikers who had passed us; they were real people who understood the spirit. So, too, the tourists and cafe staff who saw the signs on our rucksacks. The lads from Clacton were among those who took our picture and shared a laugh. We got helped in our quest for a B&B after refusing a "Four Sprung Dwarf Technique" bed at The Seaview Hotel (nice Orkney Ale, though).

The feet needed to be on a bed before we could enjoy our achievement. Wow, it felt good. I don't think the eating regime will continue: I won't need extra salt on my meals; nor sugar in my coffee and I'd be happy never to see another snickers bar. Yet the walk changed more than our diet. We have no idea how much it has changed us, but we know it has given us so much in the richness of life. Our wonderful kingdom will now be seen with bigger eyes. We have needed to look after each other in so many new ways, yet we always felt we could not be any closer. Well, we have just gone and done it.

1,008 miles in 81 days.

The world is within walking distance.

Thank you, my love
Jim x

Printed in Great Britain
by Amazon